The GERMAN WAY

Aspects of Behavior,

Attitudes, and Customs

in the

German-Speaking

World

HYDE FLIPPO

PASSPORT BOOKS

NTC/Contemporary Publishing Group

Library of Congress Cataloging-in-Publication Data

Flippo, Hyde.
  The German way : aspects of behavior, attitudes, and customs in
the German-speaking world / Hyde Flippo.
        p.   cm.
  Includes bibliographical references and index.
  ISBN 0-8442-2513-4
    1. National characteristics, German.   2. Etiquette—Germany.
  3. Germany—Social life and customs.   4. Europe, German speaking—
  Social life and customs.   I. Title.
  DD60.F55   1998
  943.087′9—dc21   98-7220
                                                        CIP

ACKNOWLEDGMENTS

The author owes a debt of gratitude to many people who not only helped make this book possible but also made it better. My German "editor" and cultural consultant, Holger Freese in Umkirch bei Freiburg, was not only the first person to see the book in its primordial form, but also became one of the most involved over the long term. His help and encouragement were invaluable. My two friends and consultants, the Austrian Herbert Kernecker and Robert Egloff of Switzerland, helped make the book's coverage of those German-speaking lands more accurate. Many others too numerous to mention emerged from cyberspace via CompuServe and the Internet to help with this project. Most notable among the many "CompuSurfers" in the Deutschland Online, European, and Foreign Language forums would be Maico Jäniche, a Berliner ("Aus dem grünen Köpenick") whose words often appeared on my computer screen to offer valuable information and insightful comments when I needed them. Others who helped by sharing their experience and knowledge include Bev Laflamme, Ted Bissell, Christian Feldhaus, Dan Depolito, and Geri Spang. I also want to thank many other good friends in Austria, Germany, and Switzerland who over the years have all helped me to better appreciate the rich and varied culture of the German-speaking world.

For updates, expanded information, photos, and related Web links, visit The German Way Web site at **www.german-way.com/german/**.

Cover Photos: Courtesy of Inter Nationes, Bonn/Germany and Heidi Hedstrom.

Reprinted with revisions 1999

99   00   01   VP   9   8   7   6   5   4

CONTENTS

CONTENTS

INTRODUCTION

Germany ended more than 40 years of political and cultural division in 1989. Austria modified 40 years of neutrality and entered a new era as a member of the European Union (EU) in 1995. Switzerland continued its 179-year tradition of neutrality and independence by rejecting EU membership in 1994. The German-speaking world has undergone many changes in the last several years. *The German Way* is a profile of the daily life and culture of the German-speaking people living in Austria, Germany, and Switzerland.

Germans and their Austrian and Swiss neighbors are often the victims of cultural stereotyping and misconceptions. The horrible events during the Third Reich and the aftermath of the Second World War continue to color people's perceptions of a culture that has given the world not only Goethe, Mozart, and Einstein, but also Bismarck, Hitler, and Honecker. This book attempts to offer a balanced look at one of the world's most significant cultures from an Anglo-American perspective. Do Germans usually walk around in **Lederhosen** drinking beer? Is ''The Sound of Music'' even remotely like Austria and the Austrians? Are all Swiss either bankers, watch makers, or Alpine farmers?

Stereotypes are difficult to overcome, perhaps because there is usually a kernel of truth in them. Witness the revival of an old joke about Europeans that has been making the rounds of late. According to this joke, in heaven the cooks are French, the police are British, the mechanics are German, the lovers are Italian, and everything is organized by the Swiss. In hell the cooks are British, the police are German, the mechanics are French, the lovers are Swiss, and everything is organized by the Italians.

The phenomenal "Asterix" satirical comic series pitted the indefatigable Gauls (today's French) against the bumbling Roman invaders, while managing to poke fun at the British, the French, the Germans, the Italians, and most of Europe in the process. *The German Way* concentrates on the German-speaking area of Europe, taking a more factual if no less enjoyable approach.

The German equivalent of "When in Rome, do as the Romans" is "**Andere Länder, andere Sitten,**" which actually says, "Different lands, different customs." The Anglo-American and German-speaking cultures are not as different as might be the case between, say, France and the United States, and certainly not as diverse as Japanese culture compared to Western culture. Not that there aren't some significant differences—or why this book? But beginning with our mutual Germanic languages (mother/**Mutter**, garden/**Garten**, son/**Sohn**, water/**Wasser**, house/**Haus**) and other shared Anglo-Saxon qualities (stress on the "Saxon"), you will find the two cultures have much in common. In this book, however, we will deal more with the differences to make things easier for the reader. This book is intended as an introduction that may serve to help you avoid many avoidable unpleasant, uncomfortable situations that inevitably arise from "culture shock." As you read, keep in mind these words from Germany's Shakespeare, Johann Wolfgang von Goethe: "There is nothing more terrible than ignorance in action." ("Es ist nichts schrecklicher als eine tätige Unwissenheit.")

For updates, expanded information, photos, and related Web links, visit The German Way Web site at **www.german-way.com/ german/.**

1. ABBREVIATIONS AND ACRONYMS

The German language uses many abbreviations and acronyms to cope with the extremely long words that result from the German practice of combining several words to create a new word. Thus, the word for the police responsible for solving crimes, the **Kriminalpolizei**, turns mercifully into the more manageable **Kripo**. In similar fashion, the infamous **Gestapo** derived its name from the first two or three letters of each word making up its full name: **Geheimstaatspolizei** (Secret State Police). German newspapers and magazines use **Pkw** (PAY-KAH-VAY) to save the space it would take to print the formal word for car, **Personenkraftwagen**.

German also has a long tradition of shortening corporate and organization names. The German film studio founded in the 1920s, the **Universum Film-Aktiengesellschaft**, has always been better known by its three-letter name **Ufa** (OOH-fah). **Badische Analin-und Sodafabrik**, the huge German chemical concern, has changed its name officially to **BASF**. German corporate abbreviations familiar to English speakers are also used in German, but with the German pronunciation. **BMW** (**Bayrische Motorenwerke**) sounds like BAY-EM-VAY, and the familiar **VW** becomes FOW-VAY.

Some Common German Abbreviations (*Abkürzungen*)

Abb.	**Abbildung**	illustration, figure (fig.)
ADAC	**Allgemeiner Deutscher Automobil-Club**	German Auto Club (AH-DAY-AH-SAY)
A.E.I.O.U.	**Alles Erdreich ist Oesterreich unterthan**	motto adopted by the Austrian Habsburgs, who aspired to a

worldwide empire. The Latin version is *Austriae est imperare orbi universo* ("Austria is a universal world empire").

ARD   **Arbeitsgemeinschaft der öffentlich-rechtlichen Rundfunkanstalten Deutschlands**   Germany's first public TV network/channel (*Das erste Programm*, channel one)

BH   **Büstenhalter**   brassiere, bra (BAY-HA)

BKA   **Bundeskriminalamt**   the German FBI (BAY-KAH-AAH)

CDU   **Christliche Demokratische Union**   the Christian Democratic Union, a political party

CH   **Confoederatio Helvetica**   Latin for "Swiss Confederation." "CH" is the international symbol for Switzerland seen on cars, maps, and in Swiss postal codes. Austria's international symbol is "**A**," Germany's is "**D**" (for **Deutschland**).

DB   **Deutsche Bahn AG**   German Rail, Inc. (DAY-BAY)

DIN   **Deutsche Industrie-Norm**   German Industry Standards

DM   **Deutsche Mark**   German mark, the German currency

DNS   **Desoxyribonukleinsäure**   DNA in English

dpa   **Deutsche Presse-Agentur**   German Press Agency (DAY-PAY-AH)

EU   **Europäische Union**   European Union (EH-OOH)

Hbf   **Hauptbahnhof**   main train station

ICE   **InterCity Express**   German high-speed train (EE-SAY-EH)

inkl.   **inklusive**   including (sometimes also *incl.*)

Lkw   **Lastkraftwagen**   truck, semi (ELL-KAH-VAY)

Mwst.   **Mehrwertsteuer**   value-added tax, VAT. Used throughout Europe.

m.E.   **meines Erachtens**   in my opinion

MEZ   **Mitteleuropäische Zeit**   Central European Time (CET)

MW   **Mittelwelle**   medium wave, AM radio

n. Chr.   **nach Christus**   after Christ, A.D.

ÖBB   **Österreichische Bundesbahnen**   Austrian Federal Railways

Pkw   **Personenkraftwagen**   car, auto (PAY-KAH-VAY)

SBB   **Schweizerische Bundesbahnen**   Swiss Federal Railways (ES-BAY-BAY)

SPD   **Sozialdemokratische Partei Deutschlands**   the German Social Democratic party

u.a.   **und andere(s)** or **unter anderem/anderen**   and others, among other things

UKW   **Ultrakurzwellen**   FM radio

usw.	**und so weiter** etc.
v. Chr.	**vor Christus** before Christ, B.C.
WC	**Water closet** restroom, toilet (VAY-SAY)
z.B.	**zum Beispiel** for example
ZDF	**Zweites Deutsches Fernsehen** Germany's second public TV network/channel

Business, Official, and Technical Abbreviations

AG	**Aktiengesellschaft** a corporation with shares that can be freely traded on German stock exchanges. Although an **AG** corporation must have at least five original shareholders, there is no maximum number of shareholders.
BAFöG	The Federal Education Promotion Act that provides scholarship money for university students in Germany.
DAX	**Deutscher Aktien-Index** similar to the Dow-Jones index of stocks in the U.S. **DAX** (or **Dax**) is sometimes also used (incorrectly) for the Frankfurt Stock Exchange, Germany's largest stock exchange; others are in Hamburg and Berlin.
EG	**Europäische Gemeinschaft** European Community (EC), now known as the European Union (EU).
e.V.	**eingeschriebener Verein** a registered association; usually a non-profit organization.
FCKW	Hydrofluorocarbons, known for destroying the earth's ozone layer
GmbH	**Gesellschaft mit beschränkter Haftung** a closed corporation or limited liability company that has one or more stockholders, and an initial minimum capitalization of DM 50,000 (about $30,000). Most German subsidiaries of American and other foreign companies, such as McDonald's Deutschland GmbH, are GmbH companies.
KG	**Kommanditgesellschaft** a limited partnership
KGaA	**Kommanditgesellschaft auf Aktien** a partnership in which the partners are also stockholders
oHG	**offene Handelsgesellschaft** a general partnership

Some Common Acronyms

Ecu	**European Currency Unit**, also spelled as **ECU**. (EH-KOO)
Stasi	**Staatssicherheitsdienst** the state security agency of former East Germany
TÜV	**Technische Überwachungsverein** the German auto safety testing agency (TOOF)

❁

3

2. ADVERTISING AND MARKETING

The two German public television channels, ARD and ZDF, show commercials mainly between the hours of 6 and 8 p.m. Mondays through Saturdays, and not on Sundays. On these two channels, programs cannot be interrupted by commercials. (This is, however, not the case for the German commercial networks.) Local advertisers may use only radio and print advertising, as television advertising focuses on larger regional, national, or international corporations.

Billboard advertising is more restricted, both in size and location, than in the U.S. In the 1850s the German Ernst Littfaß invented the round advertising columns seen in many European cities to this day. Offering an advertising surface of some 12 to 15 square meters, these colorful "lively children" (as these kiosks were called by one poet) announce cultural and public events as well as commercial messages.

Under an old German law against unfair competition, companies are not allowed to advertise products by offering discounts, bonus gifts, or other incentives for a special group of customers. Nor can advertisers make any overt comparisons between their own product and brand "X." In many countries such "specials" and advertising tactics are considered normal marketing practice, but in Germany they are seen as an attempt to confuse or deceive the customer. As a result, German magazine subscriptions are often no cheaper than single copies from a newsstand, and Lufthansa is technically breaking the law by offering its "Miles & More" frequent flyer bonus program. The partly government owned German airline decided to proceed with this bonus program because it was at such a disadvantage in the international marketplace.

By law German department stores are allowed only two major sales per year, the popular **Sommerschlußverkauf** in July and the **Winterschlußverkauf** in January. At other times, businesses may not cut their prices by more than three percent. In the summer of 1994 the first crack in this restrictive law passed through the **Bundestag** and **Bundesrat** in the form of a new law that made it easier for German retailers to be more competitive. But the law was watered down somewhat after resistance from German retailers themselves. This is, once again, a reflection of the traditional German "social market economy" designed to look out for the social good by controlling cutthroat competition and protecting the "little guy." But German public opinion is increasingly at odds with the store owners and in favor of more open competition.

❁

3. AMERICAN INFLUENCES

The presence of American occupying forces in Germany and Austria after World War II, the impact of Hollywood and American television, the sounds of American entertainers from Elvis to Madonna, and numerous other factors have all combined to lend a decidedly American flavor to the German cultural landscape. Europeans do not always regard this strong American influence as a good thing, but there is no denying that they are drawn to many elements of Americana. From jazz to jeans, from IBM to MTV, from Coke to CNN, Germans experience aspects of "the American way of life."

More than 70 percent of the movies playing in German **Kinos** are Hollywood films. (After Japan, Germany is the largest market for American movies abroad.) American television shows run on German television channels either directly dubbed into German ("Love and Marriage," "Golden Girls," "The Cosby Show") or as Germanized remakes of the American originals ("Wheel of Fortune," "Jeopardy," and other U.S. game shows). No less than three-quarters of the music heard on German radio and seen on MTV Europe is either American or in English. If it weren't for the announcer speaking German, the listener or viewer could be anywhere in the U.S.

American companies like Ford, General Motors (Opel), IBM, and McDonald's have been in Germany for so long they have become part of the German landscape. But companies like McDonald's are often faced with political and cultural protest they don't encounter in the U.S. Pressure from German environmentalist groups has caused McDonald's Deutschland headaches for years. German advertising and public relations often attempt to counter the attacks with ecological information.

The German love-hate relationship with American influences sometimes manifests itself in negative forms. Rolf Winter's 1990s German best-seller, entitled *American Impudence* (*Die amerikanische Zumutung*), called attention to what the author viewed as bad American influences—generalized by the term ''Coca-Cola culture''—that Germans were all too eager to adopt without question. Winter criticizes, among other things, the American ''no money down'' and ''easy payments'' attitude in domestic and international policy that has led to the giant U.S. national debt and budget deficits. He views capitalism in its raw American manifestation as a curse. This emphasis on the negative aspects of American culture such as racism, discrimination, violence, sensationalism, and wastefulness is a viewpoint not shared by the vast majority of Germans. For Winter, however, it is a continuation of the ideas expressed in his earlier book, *Ami Go Home*. Winter, like a number of other Europeans, has a tendency to make comments that begin with ''All Americans are'' or ''The U.S. always''—as if all Americans think alike and agree with everything that the U.S. government does. Fortunately, most Germans and their fellow Europeans realize that America, despite all its faults, is not the cause of all the evils of the world.

4. *ANGST*

The German word **Angst**, *fear*, came into the English language in the early 1940s. In its English, psychiatric sense, ''angst'' signifies a feeling of insecurity, anxiety, or apprehension. So it is only appropriate that the word comes to us from German, a language spoken by people who are constantly wracked by angst, and who almost seem to enjoy it.

Germans like to worry. They worry about politics. They worry about the environment. They worry about their national identity and their image abroad. They worry about the economy. They worry about worrying. It's not that Germans don't like to have a good time. It's just that they seem to be able to have a good time worrying. They enjoy discussing their worries. Criticism is a national pastime. Journalists do this on the editorial pages of newspapers and magazines. The average German does so in letters to the editor or over a beer at the local **Gastwirtschaft**. This Germanic trait is also carried on, to a lesser degree, by the Austrians and the German-speaking Swiss.

Opinion polls conducted in the German-speaking world tend to show a more pessimistic view of things than might generally be the case in many other countries. But, if challenged, the Germans, Austrians, and Swiss would tend to respond that they are merely being more realistic than the overly optimistic Pollyannas in other countries.

5. ARRIVAL

Most international travelers arrive in Germany by air. Although there are some direct international flights to Berlin, Düsseldorf, Hamburg, Munich and Stuttgart, most international travelers coming from non-European countries still land in Frankfurt am Main. Düsseldorf, the nearest runner-up to Frankfurt, handles less than half the over 40 million passengers that land in or take off from Frankfurt annually, and much of Düsseldorf's traffic is from charter flights. Munich's modern Franz Josef Strauß Airport (MUC) replaced the outdated Munich-Riem airfield in 1992. About 15 million passengers pass through MUC in a typical year. Hamburg's new terminal (1993) was designed to eventually handle 14 million passengers annually, although it currently serves only about half that number. Stuttgart's new airport addition opened in the spring of 1991, expanding an older terminal dating back to 1935.

Since the Wall's collapse, Berlin's three airports have had to strain to keep up with increased air travel to Germany's new capital city. Tegel, the newest Berlin **Flughafen**, continues to take the bulk of the traffic. Shortly after German reunification, Berlin's air traffic doubled, catching all three airports off guard. Lufthansa estimates an increase in Berlin air traffic to 25 million passengers annually by 2010. The site for a brand new airport for Berlin has been debated for a long time, but even if all goes smoothly, a new air facility could not be ready until sometime in the next century.

Smaller, but growing, international airports are also located in Cologne/Bonn, Dresden, Hannover, Leipzig/Halle, and a few other German cities, but most air passengers still pass through Frankfurt and the other larger airports. More than 110 million air travelers use Germany's airports annually, about a third of those in Frankfurt alone. Flughafen Frankfurt AG opened its new glass-sheathed Terminal 2 in late 1994 in an effort to keep up with steadily increasing traffic.

Many German airports offer convenient rail connections to the city center. The best, in Frankfurt, transports passengers between Rhein-Main Flughafen and the main downtown train station in only 12 minutes. There are yellow departure (**Abfahrt**) schedules on display on the upper **Bahnhof** level showing the times (**Zeit**), the track (**Gleis**), and the train (**Zug**). Munich's new airport is further from downtown than the previous airport, but there are good train and bus connections. The trip takes about 45 minutes either way.

Austria has six international airports, the largest being Vienna's **Wien-Schwechat** international airport. The Austrian cities of Graz, Linz, Salzburg, Innsbruck, and Klagenfurt also have airports served by Austrian Airlines and other carriers. Lauda Air, founded by the former Austrian auto racer Niki Lauda, offers flights to distant locales.

Switzerland's principal international airport is **Zürich-Kloten** just outside of Zurich. It offers easy rail access to downtown Zurich and other communities in the area. Other international airports are located at Basel, Bern, and Geneva (**Genf** in German). Swissair, a private corporation, and its affiliate Crossair both connect Switzerland with many other European and world destinations.

Customs procedures are usually very simple and quick, especially for citizens of European Union (EU) member states entering Austria and Germany. Non-EU citizens, including Americans, must have a passport for entry, but no visa is required for stays of up to three months. Switzerland has similar requirements. There are limits on the quantities of tobacco, alcohol, and certain other products that can be brought into these countries duty-free. Check with the appropriate consulate for current information.

6. AT THE TABLE

Being invited into a German, Austrian, or Swiss home is a special honor. Privacy is a highly regarded Germanic quality, making an invitation to dinner an honor reserved for good friends or special guests. A dinner table set for guests will usually include a centerpiece and/or candles.

During World War II, American spies had to be taught not to eat like Americans, or they would blow their cover. You probably won't have to risk your life because of the way you use a knife and fork (**Messer und Gabel**), but Europeans hold the fork in their left hand and the knife in their right when cutting food and eating. They also use their knives to help scoop food onto the fork. Rather than cutting their food, then laying the knife down, American style, German-speakers continue to hold the knife in their right hand while eating with the fork in their left hand. When the left hand isn't being used, as when eating soup with a spoon (**Löffel**), that hand should rest on the table, not in your lap. German-speakers, despite growing American influences, still use a knife and fork to eat foods such as pizza or fruit.

Napkins (**Servietten**) are usually cloth rather than paper. Paper napkins are considered wasteful. It is common for each family member to have their own napkin—placed in a wooden or metal napkin ring—that is re-used for several meals before washing.

Although saying grace before a meal is rare, diners almost never begin eating without the words "**Guten Appetit!**" or "**Mahlzeit!**" Your hosts will be pleased if you ask for seconds and eat everything on your plate. It is considered bad manners to leave food on your plate at the end of the meal. Using bread to sweep up sauces and

9

clean the plate is perfectly acceptable. To signal that you are finished eating, especially in a restaurant, the knife and fork are placed side-by-side or crossed on the empty plate.

When guests are not expected, the evening meal in German-speaking countries is often a light one, since lunch is usually the main meal of the day. Dinner often consists of open-faced sandwiches (**belegte Brote**), cold cuts (**Aufschnitt**), and salad (**Salat**).

7. AUSTRIA (*Österreich*)

The German-speaking world also includes Austria, most of Switzerland, tiny Liechtenstein, parts of Luxembourg, and South Tyrol (which is now politically part of Northern Italy, under the names of *Alto Adige, Trentino,* or *Provincia di Bolzano*). If you know that Austrians say **Servus** and Germans say **Tschüs**, you have only scratched the surface. Many of the cultural and political characteristics of Austria and Germany are more than merely skin deep.

The histories of Austria-Hungary and Germany may have been intertwined at times, but they are indeed separate histories. An Austrian does not appreciate being called "German" any more than a Canadian wants to be taken for an American. Austrians are pleased when foreigners know more about Austria than just Arnold Schwarzenegger, skiing, "The Sound of Music," and yodeling. Austria has contributed to the world's art, culture, and technology to an extent far beyond its present tiny size. Mozart, Haydn, Strauss, Liszt, Mendel, Mach, Freud, Klimt, Reinhardt, Kokoschka, Handke, Neutra, Wilder, Lorre, and Brandauer are just a few of the composers, artists, writers, actors, filmmakers, and scientists who have come from Austria.

Like the U.S. and Germany, Austria is a federal republic. **Die Republik Österreich** has existed since 1955, when it regained its independence following World War II and Allied occupation. Now one of Europe's more prosperous countries, Austria, along with Finland and Sweden, became a member of the 15-nation European Union on January 1, 1995.

Of course, Austria's history goes back much further. It goes back to the time of Charlemagne (742-814), known in German as **Karl der Große**, and the **Ostmark**, or eastern realm, created in 963 by Otto I (912-973). In 996 the Ostmark became known as **Ostarrichi**, the term that would give Austria its German name, **Österreich**. Under the Habsburg dynasty (1282-1918), Austria's power grew out of all proportion to its small size. The Austro-Hungarian Empire became a major power in the 19th century, extending its influence all across Europe, only to decline and disintegrate after its involvement in World War I. Between 1938 and 1945 Austria was part of Hitler's Germany. Not all Austrians objected to this **Anschluß** (annexation) by the Third Reich.

A small country, even by European standards, today's Austria (about the size of Maine) has nine provinces or **Bundesländer** and a population of just under 8 million. About 85 percent of Austrians are Roman Catholic. Protestants make up just six percent of the population, with the remaining nine percent claiming other religions (including about 10,000 Jews) or no religion.

The Austrian currency is the **Schilling**. Each schilling is made up of 100 **Groschen**. The schilling is closely tied to the value of the German mark, and is a stable European currency.

Like Germany, Austria has a federal structure. But there are differences in terminology and function between the two governments. Austria's current constitution is an amended version of one dating back to 1919-20, and it provides for more central powers than does Germany's. The lower house of the Austrian parliament is called the **Nationalrat** (Germany: **Bundestag**). The governor of each **Bundesland** is called a **Landeshauptmann** (Germany: **Ministerpräsident**).

8. THE AUTOBAHN

The German **Autobahn** has taken on an almost legendary mystique. The reality is a little different than the legend. The myth of no speed limits is countered by the fact that **Tempolimits** are a fact of life on most of Germany's highways, and traffic jams are common. Signs suggesting a recommended speed limit of 130 km/h (80 mph) are posted along most autobahns, while urban sections and a few dangerous stretches sometimes have posted speed limits as "low" as 100 km/h (62 mph). The fact is that Germany's autobahn system is an extensive network of limited-access freeways that can usually provide a driver with a speedy route from city to city.

Within six years after the completion of the first Cologne-Bonn autobahn in 1932, Germany added 3,000 kilometers (1,860 miles) of super highway to its road network. Although Hitler has often been given credit for the autobahn, the real precursors were the Avus experimental highway in Berlin (built between 1913 and 1921) and Italy's 130-kilometer *autostrada* tollway between Milan and the northern Italian lakes (completed in 1923). Although Germany's depressed economy and hyperinflation of the late 1920s prevented plans for new autobahns from being carried out at the time, many miles of roadway were built during the time of the Third Reich. Hitler saw the construction of autobahns primarily as a military advantage; its benefit as a job-creation program in the 1930s was an added plus.

Today's German autobahn system stretches 11,000 km (6,800 miles) across most parts of unified Germany. Plans to increase the number and length of autobahns and other highways have often met with citizen opposition on ecological grounds. One of the latest, a new stretch along the Baltic coast in northern Germany, has been surrounded by controversy by those concerned with quality-of-life issues versus those who see economic benefits for the eastern German region.

Austria also has an autobahn network, with some mountainous portions being built as toll (**Maut**) highways by public companies. Austria has a speed limit on its autobahns of 130 km/h (80 mph).

Switzerland charges drivers an annual fee for the use of its extensive autobahn network. A "vignette" sticker must be displayed on each car's windshield. Cars entering Switzerland without a vignette must pay at the border. If you're lucky, your rental car may already have one. If not, you will have to contribute 40 Swiss francs (about $35) to the Swiss treasury upon entering the country.

9. BEER AND WINE

The Babylonians around 6000 B.C. may have been the first to brew it, but the Germans consistently rank first or second in the world in beer consumption, 143 liters annually per capita by a recent count. The Bavarians and the Saarlanders rank as the most thirsty Germans. In the world **Bierfest**, Austria ranks fourth, downing an average 118 liters per person. The Swiss aren't even in the top ten.

The range of beer varieties is enough to make your head spin without drinking a drop: **Alt, Bock, Dunkel, Export, Hell, Kölsch, Lager, Malzbier, Märzen, Pils**, and **Weizenbier**, to name just a few. These brews differ in the ratio of ingredients, brewing temperature and technique, alcoholic content, aging time, color, and, of course, taste. While many beer drinkers are content merely to distinguish between **Dunkles** (dark) and **Helles** (light), a true beer connoisseur would never just ask for a **Bier**. At the very least you should know if you want **Pils** or **Export, ein Großes** or **ein Kleines** (large or small), or whether you want draft beer **vom Faß** or beer in a bottle (**Flasche**).

Even **alkoholfreies Bier** (non-alcoholic beer) has grown in popularity in Germany; but light beers have been slow to find a market. In Germany, **Pils** (Pilsner) is the most popular beer variety, with **Export** taking a distant second. Austrians, on the other hand, prefer **Lager**, an Austrian invention, with **Pils** making up only about six percent of the brews preferred in that country. No matter which variety, Germany's strict purity law, the **Reinheitsgebot**, dating back to 1516, dictates that German beer may contain no ingredients other than hops, malt (barley), yeast, and water.

The brand of beer offered will generally depend on where you are. Germany has few national beer brands. Despite a lot of consolidation of breweries in the last several decades, Germany still has 1300 breweries turning out excellent beers, most of which are sold only in particular regions. And, although 70 percent of Austrian beer is brewed by Brau Union AG, formed by the merger of two breweries, tiny Austria still has 360 beer brands produced by more than 60 breweries.

You can't go wrong by ordering the local brew. It will be served cold, but not too cold, in an appropriate beer glass or mug. It will display a white foam head that won't disappear in thirty seconds like that of most American beers. Austrians and Germans like to say a proper draft beer can't be poured in less than seven minutes to achieve the proper head.

Beer is such a vital part of the culture that the right to drink beer is even written into some labor contracts, and a beer with lunch in the factory cafeteria is taken for granted. The traditional beer garden is still very popular, especially in southern Germany and Austria. On summer evenings, strolling through town, you will often hear the sounds of a crowded **Biergarten** before you can actually see it. There are also beer gardens in the countryside outside of towns. But, wherever they are, the beer flows freely and the atmosphere ranges from raucous to convivial and remarkably family-like. You can see children sitting with their families at long tables enjoying the tree-shaded coolness and eating a **Bockwurst** or **Wienerschnitzel**. Although the young ones are drinking apple cider or soda, the adults are often drinking beer from a massive glass stein called a **Litermaß**. Some beer gardens have become rather yuppified, while others are more popular with college students. Some are like a family picnic, whereas others, like Munich's Hofbräuhaus, have more of a boisterous beer hall atmosphere. The Hofbräuhaus, one of Munich's more famous institutions, has its own popular beer garden in a spacious interior courtyard.

Germany, Austria, and Switzerland also produce some very respectable wines, particularly white wines. The overly sweet white wines exported in great quantities to the U.S. under names like "Blue Nun" or "Schwarze Katz" were not in that category. For domestic consumption, Germans prefer "dry" wines (**trocken**). Exported German Rieslings and other varieties have lately gained new respect among wine connoisseurs.

Germany has several major wine regions, including Franconia, the Rhine, the Moselle, and the southwestern "Badische" wine region. Austria produces some excellent wines from grapes grown in wine regions like the Wachau and those around the Neusiedler See. While Switzerland has some vineyards, its wine production is small and limited mainly to domestic consumption. Although many Austrians, Germans, and German-speaking Swiss enjoy a good glass of wine or a lighter wine cooler (**Schorle** or **Gespritzten**, a mixture of sparkling water and wine), they consume far less wine than beer or even mineral water.

Besides enjoying a fine wine with a meal in restaurants, you can also visit a **Weinstube**, a wine room, to drink wine and perhaps enjoy cheese (**Käse**) and other hors d'oeuvres to go with the wine. Before becoming full dining establishments, many restaurants were **Weinstuben**. You can recognize this origin in restaurants with names such as "Weinstube zur Traube."

❈

10. BREAD (*das Brot*) AND PASTRIES (*Konditorwaren*)

If there is one dietary element that is consistently found on dining tables across the German-speaking world, it is bread (**Brot**); and not just "bread," but the 200 or more varieties of bread and rolls baked in bakeries from Schleswig-Holstein to Kärnten. Many Austrians, Germans, and Swiss take the term "daily bread" (**tägliches Brot**) literally, buying their bread or rolls (**Brötchen, Semmel**) fresh each morning (or having it delivered) from the neighborhood **Bäckerei**. American-style white bread is reserved only for making toast (**Toastbrot**), while more serious breads like **Schwarzbrot** (dark brown), **Vollkornbrot** (whole wheat or rye), or **Roggenbrot** (rye) are eaten with meals or even *as* a meal.

There is nothing as alluring to the palate as those glorious institutions, the **Café** and the **Konditorei** (con-DIT-o-rye). In Austria the **Café-Konditorei** combines the best of both. This wonderful institution serves dessert and coffee at any time of the day. Your nose will usually detect a **Konditorei** or a **Café** before your eyes do. Just home in on the wonderful aroma of fresh-roasted coffee, and soon you will see a glass case containing a mind-boggling assortment of tantalizing pastries. And don't forget to try a **Kaffee mit Sahne** (coffee with whipped cream)! Unfortunately, this is no place for calorie counters. A particular advantage of the **Konditorei** is that the goodies are on display. Even though there is a menu, you have the option of just pointing at any item you would like.

11. BUSINESS (*Wirtschaft*) IN THE GERMAN-SPEAKING WORLD

German, Austrian, and Swiss business concerns are known throughout the world. Volkswagen AG is the largest manufacturer of automobiles in Europe and one of the biggest firms in Germany. Adidas AG, founded by a German, is one of the most important makers of sportswear in Europe. Nestle AG, most famous for chocolate, is Switzerland's best-known food and beverage concern, and next to Swissair and Rolex, one of the corporate names most readily associated with Switzerland. But well-known giants like these make up less than ten percent of the companies in the German-speaking business world. Most German firms are small to medium-sized concerns, known in German as the **Mittelstand**. There is no direct English equivalent for *Mittelstand*, a term that goes back to feudal times. The German word refers not only to small and medium-sized businesses, but also to a common work ethic and to the middle-class business people who employ about two-thirds of the German work force. Although the *Mittelstand* was virtually eliminated in communist East Germany, it has existed in the German lands for centuries. Today, the *Mittelstand* accounts for about half of the total industrial production of Germany alone.

It may come as a surprise to learn that business and business people in German cultures are not usually accorded the same admiration and respect they might receive from the typical admirer of the entrepreneurial spirit and business acumen. This is particularly true in Germany, where the public's regard for business has sunk to all-time lows, and where only seven percent of adult Germans own stocks (Britain: 20 percent; U.S.: 35 percent). Germans also display their characteristic aversion to risk-taking by having only five to six percent of their savings invested in shares or mutual funds, only half of the rate in the 1970s. German companies that offer employees stock in their own company have had difficulty attracting more than 15 percent participation, while an average of 50 percent of workers in France and the U.S. take advantage of such stock options.

Until recently, basking in the glow of the German "economic miracle" (**Wirtschaftswunder**) in the decades following the 1950s, corporations and business people had quietly gone about their business, with little concern for their image or business realities. There were, in fact, no German words for "image" or "public relations"— they had to be borrowed from English. As a result of this complacency, and despite its apparent success and good reputation elsewhere, German business was largely a prophet without honor in its own land. In the 1980s, as joblessness increased and German innovations such as **Mitbestimmung** (co-determination), designed to increase industrial harmony and to reduce strikes, began to lose their luster, German business lost more esteem. In fact, some top German business people became the targets of terrorist attacks by extremists who believed the business leaders and their companies were harming society. The head of Deutsche Bank (Germany's largest), Alfred Herrhausen, was assassinated by a bomb that destroyed his armored Mercedes in 1989. The fact that he and his company felt the need for an armored vehicle is itself an indicator of the climate of the time. (For more about the **Terrorism** see **Point 71**.) Germany's long history of distrust of business has helped keep such negative attitudes alive. This history may also help account for the "social market economy" model present in all three German-speaking countries. In this model, a mix of private enterprise and government-controlled operations ensures that business is "socially responsible."

Following German reunification, the debate about Germany's

economy, the third largest in the world, heated up. Anti-business terrorism continued when the head of the **Treuhandanstalt** (trustee agency) was assassinated in 1991. (For more about the **Treuhand** see **Point 74**.) In the mid-1990s, as some of Germany's best-known corporations began cutting jobs by the thousands, and chancellor Helmut Kohl's government was coming under increasing criticism for the poor state of the economy, Kohl felt moved to tell his fellow Germans that they could not continue to live in "a collective amusement park." He berated his constituents for being "soft" and urged them to get to work and renew the "**Standort Deutschland**"— roughly, "Germany as a place to do business."

In response, Kohl's critics pointed out that the German government was part of the problem. German business was suffering under the burden of too much taxation, too much red tape, too much government spending. According to Kohl's critics, over-regulation was making the cost of doing business in Germany too high. The over-valued mark was another serious problem that the government had been too slow to address. The widely-publicized Steffi Graf tax-cheating scandal was just another symptom of what many believe to be Germany's misguided tax policy. Most famous, wealthy Germans, from Boris Becker to Claudia Schiffer, had long ago moved to Monaco or some other tax haven to avoid the kind of problems with the **Finanzamt** that landed Steffi Graf's father/business manager in jail. Even less prosperous Germans were moving their money to Luxembourg and Switzerland to avoid the German tax collector.

Others pointed out that German unions and employers—even the German psyche—were also to blame. There was not enough imagination and risk-taking; there was too little investment in research and development, and German workers were earning high wages for few hours—an average 38.5 hours per week and six weeks vacation plus 12 paid holidays a year. As a matter of survival, German businesses have been fleeing Germany in recent years for lower costs in other countries, including the U.S., Poland, and the Czech Republic.

About the only thing that everyone agrees on is that German business and industry need to become more competitive. And lately the Germans have been moving in that direction; the trend is for less direct government involvement. The privatization of former state monopolies such as radio and television, the railroad, the postal service, and Deutsche Telekom is a move away from the old German mind-set. Austria and Switzerland, with their smaller markets and lower levels of competition, are more reluctant to abandon government control and the social market economy in these sectors. Austria, in particular, values its tried and true ÖIAG (Österreichische Industrieholding AG), a type of government holding company that controls oil (Austria has both oil and natural gas resources), steel, chemical and other heavy industries.

But, make no mistake, German, Austrian, and Swiss companies play a vital role in the European and world economy. Among the more influential companies are Germany's Bayrische Motoren Werke (BMW), Daimler-Benz AG (Germany's largest), Allianz Versicherungs AG (insurance), Continental (second only to France's Michelin in tires), Siemens, Porsche, Adidas, BASF, Hoechst (chemicals), Braun, Bayer, Tengelmann (supermarkets); Switzerland's Nestle, Swissair, Sandoz (pharmaceuticals), Rolex, Swatch, Tag-Heuer (watches); and Austria's Steyr-Daimler-Puch AG and Austrian Airlines.

American companies, such as Coca-Cola, McDonald's, and Eastman Kodak, whose profits outside the United States account for about half of each corporation's total, have long had a presence in German Europe. Chrysler entered into a joint venture near Graz, Austria, in 1992 to manufacture minivans and the popular Jeep Cherokee for the European market. AT&T, Sprint, and MCI have or are planning joint ventures in Europe, including in the German-speaking countries.

German companies have also established a noticeable presence in the U.S. German Allianz owns Fireman's Fund Insurance, Tengelmann owns the large A&P supermarket chain, Continental AG owns General Tire and Continental Tire. Miles Laboratories, one of the largest U.S. pharmaceutical concerns, was originally a subsidiary of Bayer AG in Germany. In 1995 Miles changed its name back to Bayer, reclaiming a famous trade name Bayer had lost in North America following World War I. It is often difficult to tell the players without a scorecard. How many Americans know that Burger King is owned wholly by a British company, or that the Mohn family in Germany (worth about $4.4 billion), in addition to owning the world's second-largest media colossus, Bertelsmann (Time Warner is first), also holds RCA Records and the Bantam Doubleday Dell publishing group in the U.S.? Almost a third of Clorox is controlled by the Henkel family's (worth $4.9 billion) Henkel KGaA, the fourth-largest chemical company in Germany.

12. BUSINESS STYLE

In dealing with German-speaking business people it is wise to keep at least three Germanic cultural characteristics in mind: (1) a deep respect for personal privacy and formality, (2) a strong regard for hierarchy and proceeding through "proper channels," and (3) a desire for detailed, logical, and frank information. Violation of any one of these cultural principles could prove disastrous in business.

Americans like to promote an "open door" policy in their offices; Germans do not. In Germany closed office doors are a symbol of the compartmentalization and desire for privacy seen in many aspects of German life. Even after working together for many years, office workers will continue to address each other with the formal **Sie** (you) and **Herr** or **Frau** so-and-so in the workplace. This does not mean they are not on friendly terms; it merely reflects the Germanic respect for privacy and the recognition of two separate spheres of life—the world of work versus that of close friends and family. Although there are exceptions in larger firms and in more modern office buildings, German offices often appear rather spartan to those accustomed to a more "cozy" or "homey" work area. In recent years some firms in Austria, Germany, and Switzerland have begun to break down the rigid hierarchy and strict separation of home and work by adopting a less formal, more "American" management approach; but this is still the exception, not the rule.

Americans tend to want to "get to the point" and may often be impatient with bureacracy and hierarchy. They want to keep the lines of communication open and avoid red tape. German-speakers are usually very uncomfortable with violations of "proper procedure" and their sense of order and structure. They want information (and lots of it), but they want it to follow proper channels and go through the accepted business chain of command. They don't like surprises in the form of last-minute changes, business calls at home, going over someone's head, or broken appointments. This need for order and conformity helps explain why German managers often share one failing with their American counterparts: the tendency to put rules and procedures before people. This Germanic compulsion for structure works two ways: (1) it can lead to secrecy and hinder the sharing of information, one of the more common problems in German business, or (2) it can help avoid misinformation and errors.

French, Japanese, American, and other non-German business people often complain that German-speakers want to provide too much information during business dealings. Sometimes it seems as if they will never get to the point. But Germans want all the facts, including historical background, and they may go far beyond what others might consider adequate in their data gathering. To some this drive for detail may seem pedantic, but to the German-speaker it means he or she is just being thorough. German-speakers may take a long time to reach a decision, but once they do, they will stick to it. Changing a decision once it has been made is rare. Knowing this, business people must make sure no information has been left out. The German news weekly *Der Spiegel* provides a good example. A story that might have taken up one page in a comparable American publication will usually fill three or four pages in *Der Spiegel*. Many Germans are critical of the content and success of American-style news magazines such as *Focus*, because these newer German weeklies are seen as lacking in-depth information.

13. CALENDAR

In Europe the week begins with Monday (**Montag**). On calendars and watches that indicate the days, the German days of the week are often indicated by these two-letter, musical-like abbreviations: **Mo, Di, Mi, Do, Fr, Sa, So** for **Montag, Dienstag, Mittwoch** (middle of the week equals Wed.), **Donnerstag, Freitag, Samstag, Sonntag**. Saturday is also called **Sonnabend** (Sunday eve) in northern Germany. This Monday-first format has the advantage of showing the two weekend days together, instead of split up, as on American calendars.

For North Americans, another unusual feature of some German calendars is the vertical format, in which the days of the week are listed on the left from top to bottom (with **Montag** first, of course). The dates also run vertically from top to bottom, so that each week of the month is represented by a vertical column. The illustration below shows a typical German vertical-week calendar format for the month of June.

JUNI					
Montag		7	14	21	28
Dienstag	1	8	15	22	29
Mittwoch	2	9	16	23	30
Donnerstag	3	10	17	24	
Freitag	4	11	18	25	
Samstag	5	12	19	26	
Sonntag	6	13	20	27	

When reading or writing a date in German, Americans need to remember that Europeans, along with most of the world outside of North America, write numerical dates with the day rather than the month first. Thus the written form of **June 7, 1995** might be **6/7/95** in the U.S., but is **7.6.95** in Germany and the rest of Europe (**7/6/95** in Great Britain). Notice the German use of periods or dots instead of the Anglo-American slashes or dashes. This information is important for Americans who don't want to mistakenly interpret **2.7.96** as February 7, 1996 when it is actually July 2, 1996.

A date such as **February 3, 1945**, would be written **3. Februar**

1945 in German. This corresponds closely to British English and the U.S. military style of writing dates (**3 February 1945** or **3rd February 1945**). Notice the absence of a comma before the year in German dates.

14. CINEMA: GERMAN-LANGUAGE FILM PRODUCTION

The Austrians, Germans, and Swiss, like many of their European neighbors, offer government subsidies to their filmmakers in an effort to encourage domestic motion picture production. Europeans, including the Germans, have traditionally tended to regard filmmaking as an art rather than a business. Because the resulting European films are often limited-budget, intellectually challenging productions that lack the Hollywood big-star, action/blockbuster formula, their mass appeal has been limited.

German film awards such as **Der goldene Bär** (The Golden Bear) awarded at the Berlin International Film Festival (**Berlinale**), as well as other European awards (Cannes, the ''Felix,'' Venice), have been created in an attempt to compete with the American Academy Awards (''Oscar'') and to call attention to German and European film. The first Berlinale film awards took place in 1951. But even the Berlinale features many U.S. productions.

It is ironic that the German film diet of today is predominantly American, especially in light of Germany's historical role in world cinema. Almost from the first days of motion pictures, both the Austrians and Germans were at the cinematic forefront, exerting great influence over the medium. Although the first paid public showing of a movie is generally credited to the Lumière brothers in Paris in December 1895, the world's first public demonstration of moving pictures took place in Berlin almost two months earlier. But German inventor Max Skladanowsky's ''Bioscop'' would prove to be impractical for widespread use. Nevertheless, Berlin soon became the center of Germany's fledgling film industry, and by 1905 there were 16 movie theaters in the city. In 1907 "**Der Kinematograph**"—a weekly journal for "the entire art of projection"—published its first issue, a tradition that endured until 1934.

Austrian and German film actors, cinematographers, and directors were pioneers in the new film art. Hollywood would not be what it is today without this Austrian and German impact. Even if non-German names like Bergman, Fellini, Truffaut, and Kurosawa are more famous in the world of international cinema, German and Austrian directors such as Fassbinder, Sternberg, Lang, Lubitsch, Murnau, Petersen, Preminger, Wilder, Wenders, and others (some of whom are still alive and working) have had an incalculable effect on American movie making. The New German Cinema is known to many film buffs, though there is no "school" of Fassbinder, Wenders, or Herzog as there is of the French Truffaut or the Italian Fellini.

In the dozen years between 1920 and 1932, the so-called "Golden Age" of early German cinema, before the Nazis ruined its reputation, German cinema led the way for future filmmakers. Beginning with the great pioneering silent films of the 1920s, such as *Metropolis, Nosferatu,* and *Das Cabinet des Dr. Caligari,* and continuing with the advent of sound after 1929—*Der blaue Engel, Die Drei von der Tankstelle, M*— German film became a model for a distinctive technique and style of filmmaking. Borrowing from the Germans, Hollywood adapted sound techniques, lighting, storytelling, and set design. German expressionistic films such as *Caligari* and *Metropolis,* which were not great commercial successes in their time, became the artistic forerunners that led Hollywood from flat lighting and mundane settings to what would become the more artistic light and shadow of *film noir.* In the 1920s and 1930s, directors like Ernst Lubitsch, Billy Wilder, and others left Europe for Hollywood. Even today, lured by bigger budgets and better opportunities, German directors continue to move to Hollywood after getting started in Germany. Roland Emmerich (*Stargate, Independence Day, Godzilla*) and Wolfgang Petersen (*Das Boot, In the Line of Fire, Air Force One*) are two of the most successful.

Austria has contributed well-known actors like the bug-eyed Peter Lorre (*Casablanca, Maltese Falcon, 20,000 Leagues Under the Sea*) and great directors such as Fritz Lang (*Fury, M, Metropolis, Rancho Notori-*

ous), Otto Preminger (*Anatomy of a Murder, The Cardinal, Exodus, Laura*), and Billy Wilder (*Double Indemnity, The Apartment, Some Like It Hot, Witness for the Prosecution*). Fred Astaire, born Frederick Auster-litz in Omaha, Nebraska, was the son of Austrian parents.

The teutonic sex symbol Marlene Dietrich (1900-1992), who be-came an American citizen in 1939, perhaps more than any other single figure, exemplifies the vital role played by Germans and Austrians in the history of film acting. Beginning in 1930, with her groundbreak-ing portrayal of the sultry *femme fatale* in *The Blue Angel* (*Der blaue Engel*), Dietrich's film career spanned more than half a century from the earliest days of talking pictures into the age of Technicolor and Cinemascope. Dietrich's 1992 death in seclusion in Paris came after a very public life that saw her starring in a western comedy with Jimmy Stewart (*Destry Rides Again*, 1939), entertaining U.S. troops during World War II, and performing on stage in Las Vegas in the 1950s—a flashback to her early days on the cabaret stage in Berlin. The late German actor Gert Fröbe (1913-1988), best known as the villainous Goldfinger, and the Austrian Klaus Maria Brandauer (*You Only Live Twice, Out of Africa*) have both enjoyed success in German and American movies. Of course, the Austrian Arnold Schwarzeneg-ger is in a cinematic class all by himself. (See also **Point 50, Movies: the Hollywood Factor**)

15. CLIMATE

Climate affects culture. Over the centuries, the long, gray German winter has led to a culture that is more somber and introspective than those in sunnier climes. Temperatures are usually low and pre-cipitation high, even in Switzerland and Austria, the southernmost German-speaking lands. They lie in the same latitudes as northern Maine or Washington state in the U.S. Zurich is about as far north as Tacoma, Washington. Most of Germany is above the 49th parallel that divides the U.S. and Canada. Germany's new capital, Berlin, is further north than Calgary, Alberta. In addition to the northern latitude, the moderating influences of the Atlantic and the North and Baltic seas tend to produce a climate that is generally without extremes. Daytime temperatures in the summer usually range between 65 to 80 degrees Fahrenheit. The winter temperatures may range from 30 to 40 degrees during the day. (Temperatures in Europe are measured in Celsius. A reading of 20 degrees Celsius equals 68 degrees Fahrenheit.)

Berlin's average daily high in the summer is 74 degrees Fahrenheit. The average July low is 55. The highest temperature ever recorded there in the summer was 96 degrees. In January the average Berlin high is 36 degrees, the average low 26, but the mercury has dropped as low as 15 below zero. In Vienna, several hundred miles further south, the average temperatures are not very different, with the thermometer recording an average high of 75 degrees and an average low of 59 in July. The winter averages for Vienna are almost identical to those in Berlin. Naturally, in Alpine areas and in some lower regions the temperatures will be cooler or warmer than the averages, but weather extremes are rare.

The average annual rainfall is 23.1 inches in Berlin and 25.6 inches in Vienna. Occasionally, there may be a summer drought, but it usually rains regularly year-round in northern Europe. An umbrella or a raincoat is a necessity. In the winter, snow falls occasionally, but heavy accumulations are unusual except in mountainous areas. In the Alps the winter snow is the delight of skiers on the slopes in Austria, Switzerland, and Bavaria. Otherwise, European and German winters typically can be depressingly gray and monotonous. Springtime and fall are usually quite changeable and unpredictable, with snow or rain one day and sunny skies the next. Summers are usually on the cool side, often with daytime temperatures in the low 70s or upper 60s. But some summers can also make Germans wish they had more air conditioning, forcing them to seek refuge in swimming pools, beer gardens, department stores, or movie theaters.

It is during such summers that one discovers little details about the German culture. On a sweltering train the window remains closed because Germans seem to believe that a draft will kill you quicker than heat prostration. If you open the window when a train is stopped at a station, a German passenger will have closed it by the time the train reaches a speed of ten miles per hour. The modern express trains are, of course, air conditioned year round.

During cold weather (which could also be during the summer) it is common in many German homes to heat only certain rooms, conserving energy. This could perhaps explain the German compulsion to shut any open door. On the other hand, at night Germans are likely to sleep with open windows for fresh air. But remember that German windows are built like a fine car, opening two different ways, either tilting inward to allow air in but blocking access to intruders, or swinging completely open. Further security is provided by **Rolläden**—the built-in roll-down metal shutters with holes for ventilation. These armored windows are the German answer to air conditioning.

16. THE COURT SYSTEM

Germany has five different categories of courts. In addition to the regular criminal courts mentioned below, there are special courts that hear only certain kinds of cases. These specialized courts might be local, state, or federal courts. Labor courts deal only with union and employer/employee disputes. Administrative courts handle cases of administrative law—usually cases where a citizen has a complaint about how some authority has treated him or her. The fiscal courts deal with tax law, while the social courts deal exclusively with social security matters. Each **Bundesland** also has a state supreme court or **Landesverfassungsgericht**.

German lower courts do have an element that resembles a jury but which is also quite different. In a trial before such a court, the appearance of two private citizens who serve as lay judges (**Schöffengericht**), is reminiscent of the Anglo-Saxon jury. But these lay judges are much more than mere jury observers. They sit with the professional judges, ask questions, and play an active role at various points in the trial. In local courts (**Amtsgerichte**), similar to municipal or

27

county courts in the U.S., the two lay members of the **Schöffenge-richt** outnumber the one judge. Although technically they are permitted to overrule the judge, they rarely do so.

Besides the **Amtsgerichte**, which handle less serious criminal offenses, the German court system has district courts (**Landgerichte**) and courts of appeal (**Oberlandesgerichte**) that handle more serious cases. A typical **Landgericht** has a panel of three state justices and two lay judges. The several courts of appeals, located only in large cities, have judicial panels with either three or five professional judges. In addition to taking on appeals from lower courts, the **Oberlandes-gericht** is the venue for hearing serious criminal cases for the first time.

The German supreme court is the Federal Constitutional Court (**Bundesverfassungsgericht**) in Karlsruhe. This court is the final arbiter in any German legal appeal. It sometimes makes law by the force of its decisions, often in controversial cases such as banning political parties as unconstitutional, or ruling on how and where German troops may be stationed. Eight of the Constitutional Court's 16 judges (in two panels of eight judges each) are elected to a single twelve-year term by the **Bundestag** (lower house), the other half by the **Bundesrat** (upper house).

Following several recent controversial judgments handed down by German courts, many Germans have begun to question the wisdom of their judges. Some are asking if German justice has become just a little too soft on crime. When the man who put a knife in Monica Seles' back during an April 1993 tennis tournament in Hamburg was given a sentence of two years probation, Seles' German rival Steffi Graf said, "This will be yet another reason for those abroad to shake their heads in disbelief." Many Germans shared her frustration over the light sentence against Günter Parche. After an appeals court reaffirmed the original sentence in March 1995, many Germans agreed with Seles when all she could say was, "I don't understand it." The finding that Parche had an "abnormal personality structure," no prior criminal record, and that he had only wanted to "punish" Seles (for defeating Steffi Graf) rather than actually kill her, were apparently grounds enough for the two-year suspended sentence.

(See also **Point 59, The Prison System**, and **Points 17** and **18** for more on **Crime and Punishment**.)

17. CRIME AND PUNISHMENT: THE LAW

The constitutions of Austria, Germany, and Switzerland each guarantee citizens basic rights under a system of written law. Dating back to Roman law, the legal and judicial systems in the German-speaking countries may differ in the details, but are generally similar. In this section, we will primarily look at the justice system of the Federal Republic of Germany.

It wasn't until 1871, with the creation of Bismarck's Prussian **Reich**, that a "modern" German criminal code was formulated. Prior to that time, German law was as fragmented as the land itself. Today's German legal code is a revised version of the 1871 **Reichsstrafgesetzbuch** and the 1877 Code of Criminal Procedure (**Strafprozeßordnung**). The legal abuses of the Third Reich led to a desire for even stronger safeguards. After 1949 and the creation of the **Bundesrepublik**, the Prussian codes were substantially modified to conform with the German constitution's guarantees of basic human rights; the first 19 articles of Germany's **Grundgesetz** are similar to the Bill of Rights in the U.S. Constitution. Since 1949, the German criminal code has been revised to provide for probation (1953) and to create a system of fines for a range of offenses and a speedier process for handling minor offenses without an actual court appearance (1970). Germany has also been a world leader in data protection laws (**Datenschutz**), passing legislation in 1977 and 1990 protecting citizens against the misuse of private information stored on computers. Since German unification, the different law codes of the two former halves of Germany have also been unified, with the western German **Grundgesetz** and criminal codes applying to all of Germany. But, as in other areas of life, not all the differences that arose over the past 45 years have been completely resolved. Some discrepancies still exist in the court system and in several other legal areas.

All of the German-speaking countries have outlawed capital punishment. And there is no trial by jury, in the American sense. Although there has been an increase in crime in Germany over the last
decade, the rate for most types of crimes is still far below that of the
U.S., and the number of serious crimes, such as murder and rape,
has remained relatively constant. The opening of Germany's eastern
borders in 1989 has led to an increase in smuggling and organized
crime. A recent government report indicated that a third of these
crimes involved illegal drugs and that almost 60 percent of the suspects
were non-Germans.

Those arrested for a crime in Germany are presumed innocent
until proven guilty. (The Napoleonic Code used in France and Britain
assumes one guilty until proven innocent.) Proof beyond a reasonable
doubt, the right to a trial in open court, the principle of double
jeopardy (you can only be punished once for a crime), equality before
the law, the right to know the charges against you, equal access to
evidence material, and other basic principles of the rights of the ac-
cused are integral parts of the German justice system.

As in all countries, the ideal and the actual practice of justice
may not be the same. A recent survey found that an average of 68
percent of Germans felt that not all citizens were treated equally
under the law. On the question of their satisfaction with the administration of justice, 40 percent of the Germans surveyed indicated they
were satisfied, while 41 percent said they were not. Almost 20 percent
were undecided. (See also **Point 59, The Prison System**, and **Points
16** and **18** for more on **Crime and Punishment**.)

18. CRIME AND PUNISHMENT: LAWYERS

Why is a German version of "L.A. Law" not likely to appear on
German TV, even if the American TV series was popular in its
German-dubbed form? While there are several popular German television productions featuring detectives and inspectors, why is there
no German counterpart to the character of Perry Mason? The answer

is evident for anyone who has ever witnessed a German trial (**Prozess, Hauptverfahren**), which lacks the drama of cross-examination, the tension involved in convincing a jury, and other American courtroom elements. The American-style suspense and tension between the prosecution and the defense are not necessary because a German **Staatsanwalt**, or public prosecutor, unlike an American district attorney, is expected to remain neutral, methodically and objectively investigating the crime in the interests of the defendant and the people respectively.

Trials are not conducted before a judge and jury but before a panel of judges. Professional judges are appointed, usually for life, and are independent of any influence from other branches of government. The prosecuting and defense attorneys do not battle each other in an effort to convince a judge or jury. Instead, the judges themselves actively participate in questioning witnesses and discussing the evidence. Rather than presiding over the trial in silence, German judges, not lawyers, dominate the trial proceedings by asking most of the questions. The defense attorney is there to look out for the legal interests of his or her client; the prosecuting attorney is there to look out for the interests of the people. Perry Mason would not be happy in a German court. (See also **Point 59, The Prison System**, and **Points 16** and **17** for more on **Crime and Punishment**.)

19. CULTURE

The cultural influences of Austria, Germany, and Switzerland in the arts, literature, music, philosophy, science, and other fields have been a significant part of the European cultural tradition. (For some of the famous names of Germanic culture see **Point 27, Famous Austrians, Germans, and Swiss**.) In the early 1800s, it was Wilhelm von Humboldt of Berlin who made research one of the foundations of Prussian university reform. His brother Alexander traveled across half the world gathering detailed knowledge of hitherto unknown flora and fauna. But German contributions are not limited to the distant past.

Germans Erwin Neher and Bert Sakmann received the 1991 Nobel Prize for Medicine for their research in cellular biology. Nobel awards in physics and chemistry also went to Germans in 1988 and 1989.

In the arts, the **Bauhaus** school of design in Dessau and Weimar had an impact on art, architecture, and industrial design that spread far beyond the borders of its German homeland. During the Nazi era many Bauhaus artists and designers left Germany for exile in the U.S. and elsewhere. Bauhaus architects Walter Gropius and Ludwig Mies van der Rohe came to the United States, where they became famous for their architectural creations. More recently, the German architect Helmut Jahn has set up his international practice in Chicago. The towering, pencil-like Trade Fair Tower, the **Messeturm**, is his landmark addition to the Frankfurt skyline.

Another German, symphony director Kurt Masur, commutes between his native Leipzig and New York City. Not willing to give up his position as head of the renowned Leipzig Gewandhaus Orchestra (he will resign that post in 1998), Masur has also taken on the task of directing the New York Philharmonic. Germany's subsidies for cultural projects are generous—a model rarely found in other countries. Today, despite recent cutbacks, 95 opera houses and concert halls as well as almost 200 orchestras are supported by the German government.

Germany has no one theatrical center such as London's Covent Garden or New York's Broadway. Its almost 30 theaters can be found in various sections of Berlin, Hamburg, Munich, and in lesser-known towns like Bochum, Memmingen, and Veitshöchheim. This multitude of theaters spread across the country reflects Germany's historical tradition of dukes and princes who once sponsored theaters for their courts. Later, during the 19th century, civic leaders began to support municipal theaters as public institutions. Although budgets have been reduced in recent years, German subsidies for theaters and the fine arts are still exemplary. More than 400 theater companies across Germany receive such financial support. Repertoires are varied, ranging from works by Brecht to Shakespeare, from Heiner Müller to Andrew Lloyd Weber musicals like ''Cats'' and ''Phantom of the Opera.''

Music and theater festivals are a solid tradition in Austria, Germany, and Switzerland. Most take place in the summer or autumn. Vienna may be Austria's cultural center, but Salzburg, Graz, and other cities also have impressive art, opera, and concert programs. Salzburg's annual dramatic "Jedermann" performance has become world famous, and the **Salzburger Festspiele** there each summer is one of the most popular. There are hundreds of other festivals in large and small communities all across German Europe. The annual Richard Wagner Festival in Bavaria's Bayreuth began in 1876. Munich's opera festival happens each July. Freiburg's **Musikfest** features jazz, folk, and other musical forms every June. In May, Recklinghausen features its theatrical Ruhr Festival in Germany's industrial heartland. Weimar holds its Shakespeare Days in April; the festival is sponsored by the world's oldest Shakespeare Society (1864). Anything but stuffy, Weimar's salute to the Bard includes a Shakespeare "rock night," performances by guest companies, and forums for everyone.

If Austria had contributed only Wolfgang Amadeus Mozart's vast body of music to the world, that would be enough. But Austria has given the musical world much more. On Christmas Eve in 1818, the world's most popular Christmas carol, "Stille Nacht" ("Silent Night"), was first performed in a small village near Salzburg. The words "The Blue Danube" ("An der schönen blauen Donau") universally convey the lilting sounds of a Johann Strauss waltz composed in 1867. Austrian-born Joseph Haydn (1732-1809), supported by his royal patrons, the Esterhazys, was part of the so-called Viennese classical school (Beethoven, Haydn, Mozart). Franz Schubert (1797-1828), Anton Bruckner (1824-1896), Gustav Mahler (1860-1911), and Arnold Schoenberg (1874-1951) were also Austrian. And many of the great non-Austrian classic composers, such as Hamburg-born Johannes Brahms (1833-1897), spent time in Vienna. Ludwig van Beethoven (1770-1827), born in Bonn, lived and worked in Vienna from the age of 22 until his death. Today Vienna remains a music capital with its grand musical palaces: the **Staatsoper** (State Opera), **Volksoper, Palais Ferstl, Konzerthaus**, and the **Musikverein**, among others. The Vienna Philharmonic's New Year's Eve concert, televised around the world, is always a sold-out event in the Musikverein's Golden Hall. And perhaps Austria's best-known musical contribution today, the Vienna Boys Choir (**Wiener Sängerknaben**), also has one of the longest musical traditions; the first Boys Choir performance took place in 1498 at the behest of Emperor Maximilian II.

20. DIALECTS

Reflecting the history of the area in which it is spoken, German is a language of great regional diversity. The area we now call Austria, Germany, and Switzerland was once a bewildering quiltwork of separate kingdoms, principalities, and duchies. So too, the German language; even today it remains a hodgepodge of dialects and linguistic variations stretching from the Danish border to northern Italy (the region of **Südtirol** in German or **Alto Adige** in Italian).

Even if the driving distance between them is only 365 miles, the German spoken by a Berliner is worlds apart from the German spoken by a Bavarian in Munich. Swiss German, **Schwyzerdütsch**, is Chinese to the ears of someone from Düsseldorf. The regional dialects of Austria, a country no larger than Maine, are like dozens of different languages, making it difficult for a Viennese to understand an Innsbrucker. The only way any of these various German-speakers are able to communicate is through a relatively standardized form of German known as **Hochdeutsch**, or High German. The *hoch* in **Hochdeutsch** refers to a topographically higher region, relative to the lower (**nieder**) or flat (**platt**) regions of the northern Germany. The term "High German" does not imply any superiority to "Low German"—the only differences are geographic and linguistic. **Plattdeutsch** or **Niederdeutsch** come from the low lands.

Ironically, in the last 10 to 15 years there has been a conscious effort to preserve local and regional dialects in the German-speaking world. Many news publications and works of poetry and literature have sprung up in dialect form. Even some dialects that had no real written form can now be seen in print. Singers and musical groups, from rock to traditional, have also released albums and songs in various German dialects. Many Austrians, Swiss, and Germans have a renewed pride in their own unique dialect. They see **Hochdeutsch** as useful and necessary, but they don't want to see their own regional cultural identity fade into a uniform, bland sameness. (See also **Point 45**, "**Language**.")

21. DINING

Defining "German" cuisine (**deutsche Küche**) today is a little like trying to define "American" cooking. What is meant by "German," "Austrian," or "Swiss" food? The stereotype Americans have of German cooking is about as accurate as the German idea of American food. Germans think that Americans drink only Coke and eat hamburgers, canned food, or TV dinners. Americans think that Germans drink only beer and eat nothing but wurst, potatoes, and sauerkraut. The fact is that "German" food has enjoyed a certain amount of diversification in recent times.

Like Americans, Germans enjoy the varied tastes of international cuisine. The meals prepared in Austrian, German, or Swiss kitchens also vary a lot by region. German cooking in general has become much lighter since World War II, and reflects gastronomic influences from Paris, Rome, Vienna, New York, and elsewhere. Any medium-sized German town will usually have some Chinese, Greek, Italian, Indian, or Turkish restaurants, in addition to a Burger King or a McDonald's. The larger cities will have almost everything. (Mexican food is still rather difficult to find.) With the influx of "guest workers" (**Gastarbeiter**) from Greece, Turkey, Italy, former Yugoslavia, and other southern lands over the years, the Austrians, Germans, and Swiss have learned to appreciate a rich variety of cooking from other lands. If you tire of **deutsche Küche**, there is much more to sample. It can be fascinating to try German Chinese food, as opposed to American Chinese food—and to discover that there is indeed a difference. (German sweet-and-sour pork is not bright red, as in the States, because the Germans frown on artificial food coloring; certain spices and seasonings are not used in the German variety.) Turkish **Döner Kabap** in pita bread is a very popular "fast food" available all over Germany.

Regional culinary differences are much greater in German Europe than in America. Bavarian food is not the same as Swabian, although these regions are "next-door neighbors." Austrian specialties like **Kernöl** (pumpkin seed oil) on salads, and the **Café-Konditorei** coffee-and-dessert palace are unique. The Swiss enjoy fondue and reclette. German cooks have long owed a great debt to Austrian, Czech, Polish, Hungarian, and other foreign influences, but never more than now with reunification and increased eastern European contact. Wild game (**Wild**: partridge, quail, rabbit, venison, wild duck) is very popular in Germany and is often seen on restaurant menus when in season. Fish and seafood are also a very important element in the German gourmet palette. If Germans want a good steak, they visit an Argentinean steak house chain like Churrasco or Maredo, found in almost every mid-sized German town.

When entering a dining establishment in Germany, it is customary to select your own seat and sit down. If the **Wirt** (owner) or a waiter notices you when you enter, he or she may greet you and suggest a seat, but you will usually be on your own. The only exceptions are some formal (and expensive) fine-dining restaurants. In some **Gasthäuser** or restaurants there is a table with a sign that says "**Stammtisch**." It is reserved only for **Stammgäste**, regular customers.

If a restaurant is crowded, Germans don't mind you taking empty seats at their table, but you should ask, "**Ist hier frei?**"—"Is this place taken?"—before sitting down at an occupied table. If you are the one being asked, just reply, "**Bitte!**"—"Please! (Have a seat.)" Once you sit down, you will usually discover that the other people at the table will very politely ignore you, although if they seem interested in conversation, go right ahead. (Some Germans may want to try out their English on you.) In some cases, particularly in informal restaurants with long tables, a party-like atmosphere may develop, with everyone joining in. Generally though, after polite hellos, each party keeps to itself despite the close proximity. But even if not a word has been exchanged, a polite "**Auf Wiedersehen!**" is usually uttered by the first party to leave the table. Americans may at first be uncomfortable with this Germanic table sharing, but soon come to appreciate how practical a custom it is when they enter a crowded restaurant.

Once you're at your table, don't expect glasses of ice water to automatically appear as in an American restaurant. And, if there is a basket of bread or rolls on the table, before you begin munching away, be aware that there is a charge for each roll or slice of bread you consume. Sometimes there is also a charge for butter, which is not necessarily provided unless requested.

Americans often find the service in German restaurants very slow. German foodservers may display a lack of urgency when waiting on tables, but it's best to remember that most Europeans consider dining an enjoyable social event that should not be rushed. In fact, it's not unusual to see people sitting at a table for hours. If you are really in a hurry, find a Burger King or a McDonald's (but be prepared to wait a little longer than in the U.S. here also). Menu items in most restaurants are prepared from scratch and may require more time. Europeans feel that good food takes time and is worth waiting for.

When the good food and drink have come to an end, diners do not wait for the waiter to appear with the check. In Europe it is considered impolite for the waiter to bring the check before being asked to do so. To get the attention of the **Kellner(in)** for this purpose one says either, "**Zahlen, bitte.**" or "**Die Rechnung, bitte.**" The foodserver may ask, "**Hat's geschmeckt?**"—"Was everything okay?" After inquiring, "**Getrennt oder zusammen?**"—"Separate or together?"—he or she will usually verify the orders with each person around the table, writing down the cost of each item consumed, total the bill quickly, write it down and place the result on the table or say the amount. (In many restaurants today, you may receive a cash register printout from the waiter instead.) The bill already includes the standard 16 percent tax (VAT; 20 percent in Austria, 6.2 percent in Switzerland) and a service charge (**Bedienung**) of 12-15%. Any extra tip (**Trinkgeld**) is optional. If the service has been good, most people add a tip of about 2-5 percent by rounding off the bill. Do not leave the tip on the table. It is more customary to have the foodserver keep the extra amount of the rounded-off sum.

22. DRIVING

When driving on the German **Autobahn**, one realizes that auto racing is not confined to famous race tracks like the **Nürburgring**. Germans, and the Austrians and Swiss, like to drive fast, and they have been in love with their cars ever since Carl Benz (1844-1927) invented the first practical motor car in 1885. The company formed by the 1926 merger of the two firms that Benz and fellow automobile inventor Gottfried Daimler (1834-1900) had created would become the industrial giant Daimler-Benz AG, Germany's largest concern. But it is Volkswagen AG, headquartered in Wolfsburg, Germany, which is now Europe's largest auto maker. Germany is the third largest producer of automobiles in the world (exceeded only by Japan and the United States) and a country that takes its driving very seriously. This is understandable when you realize that a German driver's license costs about $1500-2000, after a minimum of 25-45 hours of professional instruction plus 12 hours of theory, and such a license is good for life.

Cars marked "**Fahrschule**" (driving school) mean a student driver may be at the wheel. However, you don't have too much to worry about; in typical thorough German fashion, **Fahrschule** cars are equipped with dual controls so that the instructor can take over any time the student gets into serious trouble. The practical, on-the-road training time has to include night driving, autobahn experience, in-town driving, and a multitude of other driving situations. The test for a German driver's license includes questions about the mechanical aspects of an automobile, in addition to the usual examination on the rules of the road. But once he or she has passed the test, a German driver never ever has to be tested again to keep his or her license, not even for vision!

German and European traffic law has a few variations that North American drivers may not always be aware of. For instance, it is illegal to pass on the right on the **Autobahn**. Slow moving vehicles must always move to the right, and faster vehicles may pass on the left only. The only exception is when both lanes are moving slowly (under 60 km per hour, 35 mph), as in the frequent traffic jams (**Verkehrsstaus**). In such cases drivers are allowed to pass on the right, but at a speed no higher than 20 km per hour faster than the traffic in the left lane.

You will see speed limit signs (round) posted much less often in Germany than in the U.S. But German drivers are expected to know the law. In cities and towns, the speed limit (**Tempolimit**) is 50 km/h (31 mph) unless otherwise posted. In the last decade or so, the ''**30-Zone**'' has gained great popularity. These are residential areas with a posted 30 km/h (18 mph) speed limit to protect children and pedestrians who live in the neighborhood. On normal two-lane highways the limit is 100 km/h (62 mph). Cars towing trailers must stay under 80 km/h (50 mph). The autobahn has a ''suggested'' speed limit of 130 km/h (80 mph), a suggestion widely ignored by many Mercedes and Porsche drivers. They may suddenly appear out of nowhere, close behind, blinking their brights to move you out of their way. Not even $4.00-per-gallon gasoline can make most German drivers slow down.

In Austria, Germany, and Switzerland, children under the age of 13 are not allowed to sit in the front seat of any vehicle that has a back seat. Seat belts are mandatory for the driver and all passengers in the car, front and back.

Most of Europe, including Germany, has a .08 (**0,8 pro mille**) blood alcohol limit for drunk driving. (.05 if you are involved in an accident.) In former East Germany the legal limit for driving under the influence was zero until 1992. German law deals harshly with driving under the influence. Violators may lose their license on the first offense and must pay high fines.

Although common practice in some towns in Europe, driving at night with only your parking lights on is illegal in Germany. Headlights are required. During the day in conditions of fog, heavy rain, or snowfall, you are also required to turn on your headlights (low beam). German drivers are so well trained in the use of turn signals, they often signal even when leaving their own driveway.

It is rare to see a dented, smoking junk car in Germany. This is not just due to typical German neatness or pride of ownership. It also has to do with a German institution that is as feared and respected as is perhaps the Internal Revenue Service in the U.S. The **Technische Überwachungsverein** or **TÜV** is an agency that must approve the roadworthiness of German cars and trucks. Without a TÜV (pronounced TOOF) sticker, a vehicle can't be licensed or driven. Cars have been known to fail TÜV inspection for having a single rust spot or dent in a critical location. A broken light or a malfunctioning exhaust system would be obvious reasons for rejection. A popular bumper sticker seen on older German vehicles likely to run afoul of TÜV reads, **"Bis daß der TÜV uns scheidet."** (*"Till TÜV us do part."*)

The biennial TÜV inspection (required after three years for a new car) typically costs about DM 70 (approx. $48) for a car. The inspection must be conducted at an official TÜV inspection station or at a DEKRA station, a similar but less well known agency. An emissions test or **ASU** (**Abgassonderuntersuchung**) is required annually. This test can be done by TÜV or at any garage for about DM 40 (approx. $28).

23. ECOLOGY AND THE ENVIRONMENT

People in the German-speaking world tend to be more environmentally conscious than those in most other countries. Signs of this higher level of awareness include gray writing paper (unbleached to avoid river pollution), hall lights that turn off automatically after a few minutes (to save electric costs and energy), and ubiquitous green, brown, and yellow recycling bins (for glass, paper, and cans). Germany's Green Party (**Die Bündnisgrünen**; see **Point 35** for more about this party) was one of the first political parties anywhere to gain seats in parliament on an environmental platform. Austrian and German protesters have been active in fighting everything from the construction of nuclear power plants, to nuclear waste, to noise polluting airports. The Austrians in particular have been nervous of late about

Chernobyl-like reactors in neighboring Slovakia. In a recent survey Austria ranked highest among the German-speaking countries for the level of its general environmental legislation and policy.

People in German-speaking lands, out of habit and for reasons of economy, use far less electricity, water, fuel, and other such consumables than do Americans. They also create far less waste and recycle far more, while maintaining one of the highest standards of living in the world. Whether in the shower or in their cars, German-speakers are environmentally conservative in the most literal sense. A ranked comparison of per capita energy consumption (in 1000 kg petroleum units; lower numbers indicate lower consumption): USA, 7.7; Germany, 4.4; France, 4.0; Austria, 3.3. This means that Austrians and Germans, who enjoy a standard of living at least equal to, if not better than Americans, consume about half the energy per person that Americans do.

Not that the Germans can claim an unblemished record in matters of the **Umwelt**, the environment (literally, the "world around"). The German environmental authority was not even created until 1987, in reaction to the 1986 Chernobyl nuclear power plant disaster, and critics say it lacks real clout. The German Democratic Republic (**Deutsche Demokratische Republik, DDR**) brought with it serious industrial pollution. Even before reunification with the former **DDR**, the Federal Republic of Germany had created some environmental messes of its own, some of which continue to cause problems today. Among the first in Europe to do so, the Germans have nevertheless lagged way behind the United States in combating smog and automobile emissions by (very slowly) requiring unleaded gas (**bleifreies Benzin**) and catalytic converters. One result of this has been **Waldsterben**. (German has given the world this word which denotes the dying off of forests because of air pollution.) Over one third of the trees in the forests of Germany and Eastern Europe have already turned brown as a result of auto and industrial emissons.

Practically every German city on the map has a downtown **Fußgängerzone** (pedestrian zone) in which automobiles are **verboten**, and shoppers find an inviting mix of shops, restaurants, and department stores. These pleasant old-town (**Altstadt**) shopping areas—

often lined with lovely older renovated buildings—are a trend that has swept across Germany from Hamburg to Munich since the 1960s. The number of these pedestrian zones grew as the number of registered vehicles in Germany mushroomed from 8 to 36 million over the last 30 years. Now some town planners are calling for an even wider ban of autos from Germany's larger cities. But Germans, even while choking on exhaust fumes and smog, don't find it easy to give up their beloved cars. In adoration of the car, the Germans have spent the bulk of their public money on new roads, to the detriment of the railroad, streetcar, and bus. The result has been the same in almost every mid- to large-sized German city: traffic that can hardly move to its destination and no place to park if and when one arrives.

As traffic and air pollution worsen, the reluctance of local politicians to infringe on the rights of motorists is slowly giving way to more enlightened attempts to make German cities more livable and attractive. Some German traffic managers have visited Zurich to see how the Swiss have successfully banned cars and trucks from the city center. A few German cities, like Lübeck and Münster, have already moved to take back more of the city from the sacred car. Münster has created a bicycles-only boulevard around the city center, used by some 1400 cyclists per hour. Even Frankfurt and Hamburg, which need far more extensive efforts, have declared sections of downtown off-limits to cars. Some cities started the anti-car crusade relatively early. The 1972 Olympics provided Munich with the chance to rid its center of cars and to construct a subway system that is still one of the best in Germany. Smaller Freiburg bans cars entirely from its central **Altstadt** core, forcing motorists to stay on the periphery or to leave their cars at home and use public transportation. Berlin, on the other hand, although it has an extensive subway and commuter train network, has done little to limit city center traffic or to accommodate pedestrians, partly because of its many wide streets and boulevards. But with the Wall gone, construction sites everywhere, and many more cars from the eastern half of the new capital, Berliners find driving in their city an increasingly frustrating experience.

Other cracks in Germany's Green movement have become increasingly obvious. The supposedly model program called "**Der** grüne Punkt'' (The Green Dot) came under fire after abuses came to light. German consumers showed a willingness to pay a few extra pfennigs for products marked with a green dot, in the expectation that the plastic container would be recycled and stay out of the local land fill. But in 1993 Germany's **BKA (Bundeskriminalamt,** similar to the FBI) investigated criminal charges brought against several **Grüner Punkt** companies and found they were simply dumping Green Dot waste instead of processing it. Out of 900,000 metric tons of Green Dot plastic waste, only 200,000 tons had actually been processed.

But Germans still use less energy and create less waste than Americans. Two examples: (1) German drivers average about 5789 km (3595 mi) per inhabitant a year. Americans average almost twice that, driving about 10,012 km (6217 mi) per person. (2) In one year the typical American produces 721 kg (1586 lbs) of refuse (4.3 lbs per day), but German garbage men have to haul off less than half that amount (350 kg or 770 lbs per person, only 2.1 lbs per day).

24. EDUCATION (*Bildung*)

"**Kindergarten**" (literally "children's garden") is both a German word and a German invention. The kindergarten pre-school educational philosophy has been widely adopted around the world. It is thus somewhat ironic to discover that kindergarten in Germany is not usually part of the state-supported school system (except in former East Germany), even though about 85 percent of German youngsters between the ages of three and six attend voluntary community and church-supported kindergartens.

It was the Swiss Johann Heinrich Pestalozzi (1746-1827) who first developed many of the basic pedagogical approaches and teacher training principles that today's educators all over the world take for granted. Zurich-born Pestalozzi's ideas had spread as far as the United States by the 1860s, and his theories influenced Friedrich Froebel (1782-1852), the German founder of the first kindergarten, as well as many other educators and philosophers.

The educational system in the German-speaking countries generally follows the European model of free public education and a variety of secondary schools for academic and vocational education, rather than the American model of a single comprehensive high school for all students. Although there are some differences among them, Austria, Germany, and Switzerland all have a primary school (**Grundschule** or **Volksschule**) that begins at age six and lasts four years (five or six in some places), a secondary level that generally starts in the 4th, 5th, or 6th grade, and is divided into a less academic **Hauptschule** (to grade 10) leading to vocational education, an intermediate **Realschule** (not in Austria) leading to a technical or business school, and the academically oriented **Gymnasium** that leads to the **Abitur** or **Matura** diploma and a university education. Special education classes or special schools are offered for students with mental or physical disabilities.

In Germany and Switzerland education is primarily a responsibility of the states or cantons, and the educational system may vary from state to state. In Austria the education system is more centralized, with the federal government in Vienna bearing the major responsibility for curriculum and the funding of schools. Local entities and the nine Austrian **Bundesländer** have responsibility for school regulations and the day-to-day running of schools through school committees. Austrian school law, unlike most countries, is a part of the constitution, and any change requires a two-thirds vote in parliament. This Austrian centralization goes back to the Imperial Primary Schools Act of 1869 and Austria's imperial Habsburg history. Germany and Switzerland both have much less federal educational control and uniformity. The Swiss cantons (provinces), in particular, have their own educational systems, and the education model varies quite a bit from canton to canton. Germany's system varies less from *Bundesland* to *Bundesland*.

A typical school day starts at 7:30 or 8:00 in the morning. Classes are on a college-style schedule, with some courses offered only two or three times a week. There is also school on Saturday mornings, in some areas only on alternate Saturdays. Although the school year is ten months long and the summer vacation period only lasts about six weeks, students get many more holidays and short vacations during the school year than do U.S. students. (School days per year—

Germany: 220; U.S.: 180). The curriculum usually focuses on mostly academic subjects, even in vocational schools, with a limited offering of physical education, sports, art, and music. Religious instruction is required, but students over the age of 14 can opt out. Interscholastic sports competition is rare, though there may be an occasional track and field contest. Computer science courses are increasingly available (the Germans in particular have begun linking many of their schools via the Internet), but access to computers and other technology is still often quite limited. A 15 or 20-minute break around 10:30 am, called the **grosse Pause**, gives students and teachers the opportunity to have a snack and relax before classes start again. There is usually no school cafeteria, as the school day typically ends at around noon or 1:00 pm. (Many schools in the former **DDR** still have cafeterias.) Students go home for lunch, and in the afternoon they usually have a fair amount of homework to do.

The grading scale runs from *one* (the best mark) to *six* (*five* in Austria). Students receiving a poor mark of five or six in several subjects may have to repeat a year, but this is rare. School is compulsory between the ages of six and 15, but most students attend school until age 18 or 19 when they graduate from **Gymnasium** or advanced vocational school. (In western Germany students finish **Gymnasium** at the end of the 13th grade.)

Students and their parents have the choice of which school they want to attend, provided their grades are good enough and that the school will accept the student. This means that at age 10 they must select either a **Hauptschule, Realschule**, or **Gymnasium**. Students are not "zoned" to any particular school in a community, and in larger cities they may have a choice of several schools that offer the curriculum they wish to study. Most schools are state-run, but schools run by a church also receive public funding. Private and boarding schools (**Internate**) do exist, but they are more rare than in most countries. Education and teachers are generally held in high regard in the German-speaking world. Teachers are well-paid state employees. University professors generally have more prestige than do business executives.

Theoretically, a **Matura** or **Abitur** diploma entitles a student to automatically enter the university. While in the 1960s only about 8-10 percent of Germany's college-age students pursued university studies, now more than 30 percent go on to college. That has caused overcrowding and limitations on German university entrance, particularly in fields such as medicine and dentistry. A quota system known as **Numerus clausus** means that competition is high; students must be at the top of their class if they want to study in a popular major. Although there are no tuition fees for the universities in Germany, Austria, or Switzerland (and almost no private colleges), many students need financial assistance for materials and living expenses. In Germany, under the so-called **BAFöG** program, students can apply for financial aid, half of which is a grant and half a loan that must be paid back when the student is working in his or her chosen profession. In recent years there has been some debate about this funding and the length of time some students take to finish their studies. Compared to American undergraduates, German university students are left much more on their own, can take a lot of time between required tests, and must do more independent work. This often leads to longer study times.

In all of the German-speaking countries, educational reform has been a hot topic of discussion in recent years. At all levels, from kindergarten to university, critics have been calling for changes in the traditional way of running schools. At the same time, some educational experiments—notably the comprehensive high school (**Gesamtschule**) and the entire overburdened German university system—have come under fire. School discipline has increasingly become a problem in urban areas. Although everyone agrees that there are problems in education, not everyone agrees on just what changes are needed.

25. EUROPE AND THE EU

Austria became one of the newest members of the European Union (EU) in 1995. Germany was one of the original six countries in the EU's precursor, the European Economic Community (EEC), better known as the Common Market, which was created by the Treaty of

Rome in 1957. By 1986 the EEC had grown to twelve member nations and shortened its name to the European Community (EC), or **Europäische Gemeinschaft (EG)**. Further change came in the landmark year of 1992. By signing the Maastricht Treaty, Germany and the other eleven countries created the European Union, **die Europäische Union (EU)**. On January 1, 1995, the EU expanded to 15 members as Austria, Finland, and Sweden were welcomed, making the EU an alliance of nations with 370 million citizens and an economy ten percent larger than that of the United States.

Germany has been, and continues to be, a strong supporter of today's EU (Austria, Belgium, Denmark, Finland, France, Germany, Greece, Ireland, Italy, Luxembourg, The Netherlands, Portugal, Spain, Sweden, and the United Kingdom). Former Chancellor Helmut Kohl's government called for further expansion of the EU by accepting former East Block nations such as Poland and the Czech Republic for membership as soon as possible, a step not fully supported by several other EU countries.

Switzerland remains the only German-speaking country (along with tiny Swiss-aligned Liechtenstein) outside the European Union. Swiss voters rejected EU membership in 1994 elections (as did Norway), preferring instead to maintain Switzerland's traditional independence and neutrality. Although many Swiss felt this was a mistake, Switzerland and Norway have declined their EU invitations for now. The EU's member nations all agree on a need for unity, but they disagree on the exact form that unity is to take; some (Germany, Belgium) advocating a strong federal model, others (Britain, Spain) being less willing to give up certain powers to a stronger European Union. The German government has been a strong supporter of a common European currency, but recent surveys indicated that about two-thirds of the German public are opposed to giving up the mark for the new ''Euro.''

Germany is a signatory to the Schengen Treaty, an agreement among seven EU countries (Belgium, France, Germany, Luxembourg, The Netherlands, Portugal, and Spain) that was supposed to eliminate all controls between their borders after March 26, 1995. Originally intended to cover all EU states, the Schengen Treaty's abolition of customs and immigration controls was viewed by some EU nations as a threat to security and crime control. Even some of the countries in "Schengenland" (as it has been labeled by some) are having problems eliminating all border formalities. As a new EU member, Austria signed on for Schengen in April 1995, but it will be 1997 before border controls are eliminated between Austria and Germany.

Austria has 21 and Germany 99 representatives in the EU's 567-seat European Parliament in Strasbourg, France. EU representatives serve a five-year term. In the last several years the European Parliament has moved from being a mere advisory body to become a stronger force in determining EU laws and policies. Germany advocates an even stronger role for the democratically elected EU Parliament as opposed to the appointed European Commission.

26. FAMILY

No one would dispute that the family is a vital part of society in all of the German-speaking countries, but just what a "typical" family should be is almost impossible to define. As in most of the western world today, the family in Germany, Austria, and Switzerland is undergoing change. The divorce rate, although still less than half that of the U.S., has doubled from about one per thousand in the early 1960s to over two per thousand today (USA: 4.7). The Germanic ideal of the close-knit family, if it ever existed in reality, has taken a beating over the last several decades, as alternative lifestyles, two-income families, and the pressures of modern life increase. Spousal and child abuse are increasing problems. Drugs and alcoholism now affect German, Austrian, and Swiss families just as they do in most of the western world. There is also an increased awareness of these kinds of problems.

Germany's Federal Bureau of Statistics defines a "typical" family as one consisting of one or two parents living together in a household with at least one child. Just under 60 percent of Germans fit those criteria. Defying all efforts by the governments of the German-speaking countries to encourage couples to have more children, the birth rate has remained low since World War II except for a small baby boom in the 1960s. Despite a monthly allowance for children, called **Kindergeld**, despite other tax advantages for families with children, despite the German **Familienlastenausgleich**, a subsidy for low-income families with children, the birth rate per thousand remains at the same low level: Austria 11; Germany 11; Switzerland 12 (USA: 16). One-child or childless couples are very common, and the average number of children per family is less than two. Austria has had almost zero population growth for many years.

Although two-income families are on the rise, most women with children still stay at home and the children come home from school for lunch. Germany has very few boarding schools, and the comprehensive all-day high school (**Ganztagsschule**) has never caught on, some say because of the importance Germans attach to the keeping and raising of children in the family. Children are raised to be responsible and independent, with more freedom for teen-agers than is usually the case for American youths. Yet Germans are constantly debating the issue of **Kinderfeindlichkeit** (an anti-children attitude) in their society, frequently made apparent in signs banning children from public places and in a lack of playgrounds in many areas.

Partly because housing costs are high, older children also tend to stay at home longer. While families in the past usually stayed in the town where they grew up, sometimes in the same house, in the last decade people have become more mobile. In contrast to 20 years ago, many more Germans today live in a community other than the one in which they were born and raised.

27. FAMOUS AUSTRIANS, GERMANS, SWISS

Europeans are very history conscious. They rarely make a speech, write a book, or give an editorial opinion without an historic reference. No Austrian, German, or Swiss is considered well-educated without this historical awareness and knowledge of the important figures and events that created today's Europe.

Asked to name some historically significant Germanic figures, most people would probably first think of the infamous Austrian-born Adolf Hitler—perhaps with Einstein, Bach, Beethoven, and Mozart close behind. Unless they are history buffs or unusually well-read, many people (including German speakers) may be only vaguely aware of the wide range of German, Austrian, and Swiss contributions to art, science, politics, and technology. There are far too many famous, significant figures, living and dead, from the German-speaking countries to list here. A representative sample, including some of the most important, follows.

Hermann der Cherusker (Arminius in Latin) defeated the Romans at the battle of the **Teutoburger Wald** (Forest) in A.D. 9. A huge, rather ugly monument to Hermann's defeat of P. Quinctilius Varus' three legions stands south of Bielefeld, Germany. The Romans had difficulties bringing the Germanic tribes under control, and the Rhine remained the northeastern border of the Roman empire for 300 years. Hermann is a symbol of that Germanic resistance.

In the year 800, **Karl der Große** (Charlemagne, 742-814) was crowned Emperor of the Holy Roman Empire of the German Nation (**das Heilige Römische Reich Deutscher Nation**), the First Reich. He had become King of the Franks in 776. **Frankreich** (empire of the Franks) is the German word for France. In 963, **Otto I** (912-973) became Holy Roman Emperor and established the East Mark (**Ostmark**) which would later become Austria (**Österreich**).

Johannes Gensfleisch zum Gutenberg (ca. 1397-1468) used movable metal type to revolutionize the world with his printing press. Working in Mainz, he started printing the Bible in Latin in 1450. It took five years for Gutenberg and his assistants to produce just 200 copies. Today his 42-line Bible is the most valuable book in the world, but at the time Gutenberg lost money on the deal.

Albrecht Dürer (1471-1528) led the way to a new perspective of the world as seen through his realistic drawings of animals, a hare being one of the most famous. His *Ritter, Tod und Teufel*, in which death is portrayed as a skeleton, is yet another of his remarkable works of art.

Martin Luther (1483-1546) started the Protestant Reformation by nailing his "Ninety-Five Theses" to the church door in Wittenberg. Luther also made an enormous impact on the German language through his translation of the Bible into German.

Wolfgang Amadeus Mozart (1756-1791) began his musical career at the age of four. His musical creations in opera, chamber music, symphonies, and piano concertos are considered by many to be some of the most superb of all time. Mozart was born in Salzburg, Austria but did most of his composing in Vienna.

Johann Wolfgang von Goethe (1749-1832), with contemporaries Schiller and von Kleist, initiated the German literature movement known as Romanticism. This giant of German literature wrote the famous two-part drama, *Faust*, many other classic poetic and dramatic works, and an international "best selling" novel, *The Sorrows of Young Werther*. Goethe also dabbled in science, with his somewhat inaccurate *Farbenlehre* on the theory of color.

Jacob (1785-1863) and **Wilhelm** (1786-1859) **Grimm** collected their famous fairy tales in the volume *Kinder- und Hausmärchen*, 1812-1815. Their successful collaboration went beyond fairy tales, including a voluminous dictionary of the German language (Vol. 1, 1854), a work so vast it had to be completed by others; the last volume was published in 1960. The brothers, who rarely spent time apart in life, were buried next to each other in Berlin.

Paul Klee (1879-1940) became one of the most famous artists of the 20th century. Born in Bern, Switzerland to a German father and Swiss mother, Klee was best known for his naive/primitive style paintings, often resembling cave drawings.

Karl Marx (1818-1883) was born to Jewish middle-class parents in Trier, Germany. Following law studies, he became the editor of the *Rheinische Zeitung*. When the paper was closed down by the government, he left for Paris, where he met fellow German, **Friedrich Engels** (1820-1895), with whom he began a long collaboration. Together they wrote the *Communist Manifesto* in 1848. Marx published the first volume of *Das Kapital* in 1867, but the later volumes were edited and published after his death by Engels. Marx spent the last years of his life in London, where he is buried.

Friedrich Nietzsche (1844-1900), philosopher and writer born in

Saxony in eastern Germany, became famous for his **Übermensch** (superman) and the wisdom of his Zarathustra. His philosophy, expounded in works like *Die Geburt der Tragödie* (*The Birth of Tragedy*, 1872), *Also sprach Zarathustra* (*Thus Spoke Zarathustra*, 1883), and *Der Wille zur Macht* (*The Will to Power*, 1888), was falsely adopted by the Nazis, but only by corrupting and editing Nietzsche's true ideas, which rejected anti-Semitism, as well as German nationalistic and racist tendencies. Nietzsche suffered from physical and mental illness in his last years.

Sigmund Freud (1856-1939), the Austrian father of psychoanalysis and creator of the vocabulary of neuroses, lived to see his books burned by the Nazis before he fled Austria for London just prior to his death. His theories about the id, the ego, and psychoanalysis in general continue to be subject to intense debate. The Swiss **Carl Gustav Jung** (1875-1961) also had a great influence on the field of psychology and psychiatry. Rejecting some of the theories of his friend Freud, Jung developed analytic psychology.

Konrad Adenauer (1876-1967), the postwar "George Washington" of Germany, became the first chancellor (1949-1963) of the new Federal Republic of Germany and helped lead West Germany to the recovery and prosperity of the "economic miracle."

Lise Meitner (1878-1968) was born in Vienna, where she became only the second woman to receive a doctorate in physics in 1905. She later went to Berlin and became a professor in 1926. After the Austrian *Anschluß* of 1938 she continued her scientific career in Stockholm, working on nuclear fission, a term she helped coin. Refusing to work on the atomic bomb, she retired to England, where she died.

Willy Brandt (1913-1992) became mayor of West Berlin in 1957, was German chancellor (SPD, Social Democrats) from 1969 to 1974, and winner of the 1971 Nobel Peace Prize for his **Ostpolitik** of rapprochement with East Germany. Brandt was a popular statesman and remained influential in the SPD up to his death.

Helmut Schmidt (1918-   ) was Brandt's successor in 1974 and chancellor (SPD) for the next seven years. One of the most intellectual of all German chancellors, Schmidt speaks eloquently in both German and English and has written several books. He is still popular, appearing on television and publishing **Die Zeit**, one of Germany's most respected weekly journals.

28. FASHION AND DESIGN

The Bauhaus school of architecture and industrial design is one of the best-known symbols of German design skill. And Mercedes and its distinctive star hood ornament have combined with the Swiss Swatch concern to create the stylish Swatchmobile. But Germany never ranked high in fashion design.

This is changing as the Germans join Italian (Giorgio Armani, Prada) and American (Donna Karan, Calvin Klein) designers in challenging French *haute couture*—in both fashion and fragrances. German fashion houses such as Escada ready-to-wear and the more exclusive **Jil Sander** (born in 1943 as Heidemarie Jiline Sander) have developed a reputation for popular design and a ''hip'' fashion sense. Even in Paris, German-born **Karl Lagerfeld** (1938-   ) of Hamburg (like rival Jil Sander) has helped bring the house of Chanel back to prominence. Berlin, Germany's pre-war fashion center, has enjoyed a revival with young designers such as former East Berliners Martin Wuttke and Annett Röstel, Austrian Lisa D (who has been in the city for over a decade), and Claudia Scoda. Berlin's eastern half continues to attract young designers with its lower rents and its more relaxed atmosphere. A few years ago IGEDO, Germany's fashion organization, introduced **ModaBerlin**, a fashion exhibition that supplements the main Düsseldorf spring fashion fair—which displayed in a brand new exhibition hall in 1995.

While fashion designers like Claudia Scoda and Karl Lagerfeld often complain about their fellow Germans' general lack of a real fashion sense and a weak appreciation for their home-grown designers, they do have the sweet consolation of international success. Fashion in the nineties has truly gone international. Like its smaller rival ModaBerlin, Düsseldorf's fashionable **Kö** boulevard (short for **Königsallee**) and the

Düsseldorf fair lure not only native designers to the German fashion capital but also world-renowned French, British, and Italian designers. About a month after Düsseldorf's fashion show, many German designers will again be seen in Paris or Milan. The young American designer and MTV personality Todd Oldham was recently hired by Germany's Escada and has shown his designs in Düsseldorf. The Swabian firm of **Hugo Boss AG**, Germany's largest maker of men's clothing, is becoming increasingly international. German super models **Claudia Schiffer** (1970-) and **Nadja Auermann** (1971-) walk down the runway for various designers from Paris to New York. A former East German born in Potsdam, **Wolfgang Joop** (1944-), reigns as one of Germany's best-known international fashion kings; he is just as comfortable in New York City as in Milan or Düsseldorf. And who has photographed most of it? Enter **Helmut Newton** (1921-), a Berliner who became one of the world's most famous fashion photographers; he now lives in Monte Carlo. Newton revolutionized fashion photography in the 1970s by moving outside of the traditional studio and using natural outdoor settings for fashion shots.

29. FLOWERS AND GARDENS

A first-time visitor to Austria, Germany, Switzerland, or the once-German Alsace (**Elsaß**) region of France is struck by the spring flowers brightening the balconies and windows of almost every house. To a German **Hausfrau**, a window is naked and incomplete without a complement of bright red geraniums and other colorful floral decoration. On the inside, cacti, succulents, and other houseplants adorn the windowsills, adding cheer to the interior decor.

Even stores and shops join in this floral celebration by gracing their own windows and balconies with flower boxes in the summer. Potted plants, shrubs, and even palms line streetside cafes during the warm season. Public areas and parks are dotted with artfully arranged flowerbeds and plants of all kinds.

Although regarded by many Germans today as **kitschig** (tacky), you may still see front yards sporting one or more colorful ceramic gnomes, called **Gartenzwerge**. The lederhosen-clad **Gartenzwerg** is a Germanic phenomenon, symbolic of a love of the soil as well as of the need to stake out territory. The tradition of garden dwarfs actually came to Germany centuries ago via a circuitous route from Turkey via Italy.

Another German gardening tradition is the **Schrebergarten** or **Kleingarten**. Although no longer just a German phenomenon, these small plots of gardening heaven can be seen dotting the landscape just outside urban areas, especially alongside railroad lines all over the country. The **Schrebergarten**, named for Leipzig physician D.G. Schreber, who first came up with the mini-garden idea back in the 1860s, provides German urban apartment dwellers with a patch of green that they might otherwise be denied. German law limits the size of such gardens to no more than 400 square meters. A small cottage or shed at one end (maximum size 24 square meters) helps turn this minuscule plot of land into a weekend getaway, a flowered home away from home, and a return to nature not possible in the tight rows of apartment complexes. Local and regional **Kleingarten** associations represent the interests of part-time gardeners.

Visitors to the beautiful **Schlösser** (castles or palaces) of Austria, Germany, and Switzerland can enjoy colorful formal gardens in the French style. Modeled on the geometrical gardens of Versailles, these Germanic imitations at Schönbrunn (Vienna), Nymphenburg (Munich), and Herrenchiemsee (Bavaria) all have magnificent formal gardens graced with fountains, reflecting pools, statues, shrubs, and precisely executed floral patterns.

In many towns across the three main German-speaking countries, a floral clock shows the time with flowery numerals and hands. In similar fashion, some cities greet visitors with a floral sign of welcome (**Willkommen**).

30. FOREIGNERS AND *Ausländerhaß*

About eight percent of Germany's population is non-German, but no less than 20 percent of the population of some of Germany's largest cities are non-citizen residents. Germany's **Gastarbeiter** (guest workers) come primarily from Turkey, Italy, Greece, and former Yugoslavia. (In the eastern part of Germany, most of the guest workers came from communist Vietnam.) In Austria, there are more than 680,000 foreign residents, just under eight percent of the total population. Only about 270,000 of these Austrian foreigners are officially **Gastarbeiter**, most of them from Turkey and former Yugoslavia. In Switzerland more than 17 percent of the population is non-Swiss, some of them **Gastarbeiter** from a variety of southern European and Middle Eastern nations. In all three German-speaking countries, many of these foreigners (**Ausländer**) are people who were encouraged to come and do the work that the natives did not want to do. The **Gastarbeiter** clean the streets, collect the garbage, wash dishes, lay cobblestone and brick, work in construction or in factories, and do many other back-breaking or dull jobs. Although the **Gastarbeiter** were supposed to be temporary workers, almost 60 percent of the foreign residents in Germany have been living there for ten years or more. Two-thirds of their children were born in Germany. In good times these foreigners are needed to expand a limited pool of unskilled workers; in poor times they are resented for taking jobs away from the natives. This can lead to **Ausländerhaß** (hatred of foreigners).

If this all sounds similar to the Hispanic or Asian immigration problem in the United States, it is. In Austria, Germany, and Switzerland the same kind of resentment that may be felt towards Hispanics and Asians in the U.S. is directed towards the Turkish, Italian, and Yugoslavian workers and their families. As in the U.S., not all native-born citizens resent or dislike the foreigners. However, there has been a rising tide of discontent related not only to the once-welcome immigrants, but also regarding increasing numbers of asylum seekers from less prosperous, less democratic nations. This has particularly been felt in Germany, which until very recently had some of the most liberal asylum laws in Europe. Compounding the problems is the fact that it is difficult for foreign residents to become citizens of Germany, Austria, or Switzerland. Under the laws of these German-speaking countries, people of "foreign" blood born in the country do not automatically become citizens.

Incidents of violence against foreigners in Germany and Austria in the last several years have led to questions about right-wing, nationalistic tendencies. Since reunification, neo-Nazis in both eastern and western Germany have become more visible and more active. Sometimes-fatal arson attacks directed against Turks and other **Ausländer** living in Germany, a deadly pipe bombing of gypsies living in Austria, letter bombs sent to prominent Austrians known to oppose bigotry, and other such hate-inspired incidents demonstrate the need for more effective measures to counteract racist and anti-foreigner sentiments. Sadly, a few right-wing politicians in all three German-speaking countries have chosen to use foreigners as a scapegoat for problems such as crime and unemployment. Although the great majority of Austrians, Germans, and Swiss opposes such hate mongering, small comfort could be taken from a recent Swiss referendum in which voters just narrowly rejected measures aimed at excluding or ejecting foreigners from that country. Austrian voters rejected a recent bid by the radical, right-wing Jörg Haider to win a greater role in Austrian politics for his FPÖ party. In Germany, the Kohl government has come under increasing criticism for not taking a more proactive stand to combat prejudice, xenophobia, and their ugly results.

31. FRIENDS AND ACQUAINTANCES
(*Sie* and *du*)

German-speakers tend to be more formal and reserved than do some other cultures in conducting their personal and business affairs. As in other European languages, German has both a formal and a familiar form for "you." The formal **Sie** is used to address strangers, business associates, and acquaintances (**Bekannte**, as opposed to close friends, **Freunde**), and for most situations outside the family. For family and relatives, close friends, young children, pets, and God, the familiar **du** is used (**ihr**—"you guys"—in the plural). People in the same social group or class, such as students or factory workers, usually address each other as **du**, but white-collar workers and profes-sionals rarely do so.

Although there has been a tendency in recent years towards less formality—generally, the younger the person, the more likely they are to use **du** instead of **Sie**—visitors from outside the culture are wise not to adopt this informal approach too quickly. It is better to risk being too formal rather than too familiar. When in doubt, use **Sie**. Think of **Sie** as the proper form to use when you might address someone as Mr. or Mrs. so-and-so, rather than by their first name. Using a familiar, first-name approach in the wrong situation could be insulting or demeaning, a faux pas that one usually wants to avoid in any business and social dealings.

While the Germans and the Swiss (the Austrians less so) are often thought of as cold, and a friendship takes longer to establish, that friendship is often deep and enduring. Casual friendships, American style, are less common.

In Germanic-culture business situations, you should never use a person's first name. It is too easy for Americans or other English-speakers to falsely assume that because a German-speaker is being friendly and congenial, it is all right to become more familiar. But such premature familiarity makes most Germans uncomfortable, even though they might not say so. It is advisable to allow your Austrian, German, or Swiss counterpart to decide when or if a less formal relationship is appropriate.

32. THE GERMAN PAST

In 1995, fifty years after the end of World War II, the German past was still haunting not only Germany, but Austria and Switzerland as well. Preparations for the European ceremonies commemorating the 50th anniversary of VE-Day on May 8 raised anew the questions of guilt and responsibility that are the legacy of the Third Reich. As the debate about the meaning of May 8 raged, the German weekly

Die Zeit wondered, "Today there is so much talk about reconciliation—why in the world can't we start at home?"

Unlike perhaps any other country on the face of the earth, Germany confronts a unique and horrible past that is one of the darkest periods in world history. Many of those Germans who were only children during the war, or who were born after 1945, resent having to deal with Germany's Nazi past. But to this day, the German past affects German life in many ways. The dozen years between 1933 and 1945 impacted the German culture to a degree that may seem out of all proportion to the short span of history. But it was the degree of government-backed horror—the systematic persecution and murder of the Jews, gypsies, and other minorities—that has led to this blot on the German psyche.

No living German remains unaffected by this dark shadow on German history. It pervades virtually every aspect of German life. Whether spoken or unspoken, the issue of the Nazis and the Holocaust looms behind almost anything an individual German or the German government does. The fact that there is no German equivalent of the Fourth of July—not even any real "national day" of celebration—stems from shame surrounding the nationalistic excesses of the Nazis. To a German, even celebrating the birth of a new post-war democratic federal republic on May 23, 1949 (a date that few Germans know) seemed too reminiscent of the negative connotations of the National Socialists (Nazis). May 23 has come and gone each year since 1949 without any public commemoration, much less any celebration, in Germany.

One would expect that November 9, the glorious day when the Berlin Wall opened in 1989, would be another cause for national celebration. But that date also happens to be the anniversary of a dark event in the recent German past, the **Kristallnacht** "night of glass" when the Nazis systematically smashed in the storefronts of Jewish businesses. Because of this unfortunate coincidence, the German Bundestag felt it necessary to avoid any official celebration on November 9. Instead, October 3 became the Day of German Unity, **Tag der deutschen Einheit**, commemorating the official date when

East and West Germany again became one in 1990. October 3 became a legal holiday in 1992, replacing the older June 17 holiday of the same name (that marked the date of the East German workers' uprising in 1953).

Even neutral Switzerland isn't immune to Nazi skeletons in its closet. Besides the more recent controversy over Nazi gold and Swiss banks, in 1995 the issue of the "Swiss Oscar Schindler" came to a head. Following **Anschluß** in 1938 an estimated 12,000 Jews were turned back by the Swiss while trying to escape Nazi-controlled Austria. Paul Grüninger defied this Swiss policy. Grüninger, a chief of police in the canton of Saint Gallen, helped about 3,000 escaping Jews enter Switzerland by forging documents. But unlike Schindler, Grüninger's reward was the loss of his job and his pension. He died poor and disillusioned in 1972. It wasn't until 1993 that media pressure forced the Swiss to grudgingly admit that perhaps an injustice had been done; but there was no official pardon. There was more at stake than just the Grüninger case. The Swiss were being forced to confront the issue of tacit collaboration with the Nazis' antisemitic policies by the Swiss army and even the Swiss-based International Committee of the Red Cross. Finally, almost 47 years after his good deed, Grüninger's family received his long overdue pardon in late 1995.

The end of the Cold War, the anniversaries of D-Day and VE-Day, the growth of rightists movements in not just Germany but in Austria, Italy, France and other parts of Europe as well, have all led to greater confrontation with the Nazi past. Withdrawal of American troops from Germany has aggravated the problem. For example, as the American military prepared to give some of their Bavarian installations back to the German government, towns like Berchtesgaden were confronted with the question of what to do with Hitler's old redoubt in the Bavarian Alps. As long as the former Nazi sites were in American hands there had been no fear of Hitler's former installations becoming a possible shrine for neo-Nazis. Now there is debate over how to deal with the issue. A slightly different problem exists in Poland, formerly East Prussia, where Hitler's half-destroyed "Wolf's Lair" ("**Wolfsschanze**") is open to tours by the public.

With the opening of Eastern Europe, the site of Graf von Stauffenberg's July 20, 1944 failed assassination attempt on Hitler has become a magnet for 250,000 Polish, German, and other tourists each year.

33. GESTURES

German-speakers may not be as well known for gesticulation as the French, Italians, or Spaniards, but there are certain gestures and facial characteristics that are clearly understood throughout the German world. Some German-speakers are quite demonstrative when talking, using their hands to help express what they are saying, in a manner that generally can be understood by anyone. But some gestures may be unfamiliar to English-speakers. Also be sensitive to your own gestures; do not casually use gestures that may unintentionally offend someone. It is wise to avoid using any Germanic gestures until you are more familiar with their use.

One gesture you should be aware of, but should never use, is tapping the forehead or temple with the index finger. This gesture, most often seen on the road, roughly translated, means that someone is an idiot or is crazy. It is most frequently seen after you have offended an impatient German driver by doing something of which he does not approve. But also be aware that such gestures are punishable by a fine if someone wants to press charges against the offender. (Other Europeans use a similar gesture to question someone's intelligence, but usually tap the temple rather than the forehead.)

German-speakers also use some of the conventional gestures known throughout Europe. For instance, rubbing the thumb over the index and middle finger, palm up, indicates money. As in all of Europe, the number one is indicated by the thumb rather than the index finger. To indicate the number two, use the thumb and the index finger. Using the index and middle fingers, the American way, may cause a German to think you mean three. Germans don't cross their fingers for luck, they "press their thumb" (**Daumen drücken**) between the index and middle fingers. But don't allow the thumb to stick out too far. You then have an obscene gesture!

When you are sitting in a meeting and suddenly the Germans sitting around the conference table all start rapping their knuckles on it, they are showing their approval and agreement. This table tapping seems to be the uniquely Germanic equivalent to applause or the British exclamation of "Hear! Hear!"

Europeans, and German-speakers in particular, smile less frequently than do Americans. This is not a sign that they are unfriendly or antagonistic, but is merely a reflection of the European belief that "unnecessary" smiling is superficial and insincere. Smiling at strangers for no reason is considered silly. A smile from an Austrian, German, or Swiss really means something. So you should not take offense at the lack of a smile.

34. GOVERNMENT AND POLITICS

Austria

Reestablished as the Republic of Austria (**Republik Österreich**) in 1955 in the aftermath of World War II, Austria is a democratic federal republic with nine states or **Bundesländer**. A republic since 1918, Austria's 1955 constitution is based on one dating back to 1920. The **Bundeskanzler** (federal chancellor) is technically appointed by the president, with legislative approval. In reality, the Austrian **Bundeskanzler** holds a position similar to that of the British prime minister. The federal president (**Bundespräsident**) is the titular head of state, but has very limited political powers. Elected for a six-year term by a direct vote of the people (voting for president is compulsory in Austria), the president can dissolve parliament, helps appoint government ministers with parliamentary approval, and is the commander-in-chief of the armed forces. The legislative branch is composed of an upper house, the **Bundesrat** or Federal Council, and a lower house, the **Nationalrat** or National Council.

Austria's two major traditional political parties, the social democrats (**SPÖ, Sozialistische Partei Österreichs**) and the conservative people's party (**ÖVP, Österreichische Volkspartei**), have come under increasing criticism and pressure in the last few years, following political scandals and charges of incompetence. The main benefactor of this political turmoil has been the young, dapper, right-wing politician, Jörg Haider (1950-   ) and his Austrian Freedom Party, or **FPÖ (Freiheitliche Partei Österreichs)**, also known as "**die Freiheitlichen**" (roughly, "the freedom lovers"). Until recently, Austrian voters had been showing their discontent with the traditional parties by giving more votes to Haider. His thinly veiled neo-Nazi tendencies failed to deter voters who liked his charm and his anti-foreigner, "Austria first" platform. Although Haider managed to draw almost a quarter of the vote in two recent elections, the FPÖ has been unable to find a willing partner to form a coalition and gain a major position in the government for the party and Haider.

Germany

Between 1949 and 1990 Germany was split in half. The two Germanys were a stark symbol of the Cold War era. Less than a year after the Berlin Wall came down, on October 3, 1990, the former German Democratic Republic (**Deutsche Demokratische Republik**) or East Germany ceased to exist and was merged into the Federal Republic of Germany (**Bundesrepublik Deutschland**). In 1992, after intense debate between supporters of Bonn, the capital of Germany for 40 years, and Berlin, the historic capital, the Bundestag decided that the German seat of government would return to Berlin by 2003.

Ruling over all this change was "King Kohl," Helmut Kohl (1930-   ) of the Christian Democratic Union (CDU). During his record 16 years in office, Kohl, who became chancellor (**Bundeskanzler**) in 1982, broke the record for length of time in office previously held by Konrad Adenauer (1876-1967). Adenauer was West Germany's first chancellor for 14 years from 1949 to 1963. After German reunification proved to be much more expensive and difficult than Kohl had promised, he still managed to avoid what many thought would be certain defeat in the 1994 fall elections. Germany's other major political party, the Social Democratic Party (SPD), has had trouble gaining voter support ever since Helmut

Schmidt (1918-   ) lost the chancellorship to Kohl and the CDU in 1982. But the Kohl era finally came to an end on September 27, 1998 when German voters rejected Kohl and his CDU party for the SPD candidate Gerhard Schröder (1944-   ).

Under Germany's federal structure, similar to that of the U.S., certain powers, such as police, education, traffic law, etc., are reserved to the states (**Bundesländer**). Each **Bundesland** has its own state legislature and governor, called a **Ministerpräsident**. In Germany's parliamentary system, the 16 **Bundesländer** are represented in the federal council or **Bundesrat**, an upper house similar to the U.S. Senate (but **Bundesrat** members are appointed rather than elected), while the 660-plus seats of the **Bundestag** (federal council or parliament) are filled by elected representatives (four-year term) from the various states, similar to the U.S. House of Representatives. These representatives or **Abgeordnete** are elected through a complex dual-vote process, whereby voters have both a vote for a candidate from their local constituency and a second vote for a list of candidates presented by the parties. The purpose of the second vote is to ensure that the parties have representation in the **Bundestag** proportional to their share of the total vote, while the first vote gives the voter a choice of an individual candidate.

The **Gemeinde** or community is the local level of government in Germany. The **Gemeinde** is a city or town with an elected **Bürgermeister** or mayor. It is at this level that most of the decisions affecting the average citizen take place. The voter turnout in local, state, and national German elections usually runs between 60 and 80 percent, a degree of electoral participation that far exceeds the average 30-40 percent U.S. turnout.

Switzerland

Very few Swiss can name their country's head of government, who holds office for only one year and then slips back into even more anonymity, reflecting Switzerland's philosophy of reserving most political power to local government and the cantons (provinces). The oldest continuous government in the major German-speaking lands,

Switzerland traces its history back to 1291 and the founding of the Swiss Confederation (**Schweizerische Eidgenossenschaft**). The Confederation adopted a federal constitution in 1848 (last revised in 1874). Today Switzerland has a unique, highly decentralized structure, with most governmental power reserved to the 26 cantons and more than 3000 communes (**Gemeinden**).

The Swiss democracy is largely run by direct democratic vote at every level. The people vote on almost every matter, including every school or hospital to be built in the community. Even teachers are elected and reelected by referendum. Only important central powers like foreign relations, the armed forces, postal and monetary concerns, and other national matters are delegated to the federal government, although there has been a more recent tendency towards increased federal power. Still, the Swiss cantons and local communities continue to have much greater independence and autonomy than do local and state governments in other countries.

35. THE GREENS (*die Bündnisgrünen*)

Arising out of German enthusiasm for environmental ''green'' issues in the 1970s, the Greens (**die Bündnisgrünen**) became a viable political party at the national level in 1980. The Greens' decidedly liberal political agenda deals mainly with ecological concerns and European demilitarization. Especially in the early years, the Greens had a rather flower-child, hippie image. Green delegates refused to wear suits in the Bundestag, preferring more casual attire; sometimes they decorated their parliamentary seats with potted plants. Disagreements about how far to compromise on Green issues and what kind of political alliances to build soon resulted in a party split—one wing remained fundamentalist, the other became more pragmatic (the **Realos**). Following a decline in power, most notably in the 1990 postreunification elections when the Greens failed to gain enough votes in all the western German states to meet the minimum five percent requirement, the party decided to merge with the eastern Alliance

90 (**Bündnis 90**) party, with which the Greens had managed to win eight seats in the East. Since May 1993 the new joint party has been known as **Bündnisgrünen** (Alliance/Greens). In recent years the new alliance has managed to hang on slightly above the five percent national minimum level, with 6.7 percent in 1998 (down from 7.3 percent in 1994). Part of the Greens' survival can be attributed to their strategy of forming so-called "traffic light" coalitions with other parties. Ther term comes from the colors associated with most of Germany's political parties: red for the socialist SPD, yellow for the liberal Free Democrats (FDP), green for the Alliance90/Greens, and black for the "Union" or CDU/CSU. After their 40.9 percent victory in 1998, the SPD was forced into a somewhat uneasy red-green "marriage of convenience" with the Greens in order to form a majority in the Bundestag.

Austria's Greens have been in the **Nationalrat** since 1986, drawing an average of just under five percent of the vote. The Swiss "Environmentalists and Free List," similar to the Greens, have had between 11 and 14 seats in the 200-seat National Council since 1987.

36. GREETINGS AND COMMON COURTESIES

Guten Tag, Hallo, Grüß Gott, Grüezi, and a number of other forms of "hello" are heard in various parts of the German-speaking world, depending on the country and/or the region. But learning to shake hands is even more important than learning the proper form of "hello." German-speakers shake hands much more often than Americans. Although in recent years they do so less often, Germans, Austrians, and Swiss still shake hands in more situations than Americans. Any time people meet is generally an occasion for hand shaking—by men and women. This includes introductions, parties, and even mornings in the office. If in doubt, wait for the natives to extend their hands, but be prepared. During introductions it is proper to say your last name or the last name of the person being introduced and "Guten Tag." First names are out, a difficult thing for Americans to remember.

German-speakers value their hellos and good-byes. They even say "Guten Tag" on entering a shop and "Auf Wiedersehen" when leaving. "Tschüss" has been gaining popularity in recent years for "Bye" or "So long." Originally only heard in Germany, "Tschüss" has now spread south into Austria.

There are many subtle differences in common courtesies. Such everyday occurrences as opening doors and the question of who enters first can be different. Walking or sitting on the right of a person is the "position of honor"—thus the man should walk on the left side of a lady rather than staying on the street side. According to German business protocol, a subordinate should let the boss stay on the right. In a restaurant the man enters first, holding the door for the lady. But modern times have also come to Europe, and the younger generation worries much less about these conventions than their elders.

37. THE HABSBURGS

The House of Habsburg (**das Haus Habsburg**, sometimes spelled "Hapsburg" in English), most closely identified with Austria, became one of the world's greatest royal families by extending its influence across most of Europe for centuries—from its beginnings in 1273 until 1918. Taking its name from the "hawk's castle" (**Habichtsburg**) in the Swiss Aargau, the dynasty actually dates back to the 10th century when it had interests in Swabia, Switzerland, and the Alsace. The significant beginning of the House of Habsburg is usually dated from 1273, when Count Rudolf of Habsburg was elected as the German king Rudolf I. With the exception of the years 1742 to 1745, a Habsburg held the title of Emperor of the Holy Roman Empire of the German Nation (**Kaiser des Heiligen Römischen Reichs Deutscher Nation**) continuously from 1438 to 1806. Clever use of the Habsburg policy of expansion through marriage and inheritance soon gained territory in France, the Netherlands, Spain, and many other parts of Europe.

After 1556 the House of Habsburg became a house divided, splitting into a Spanish and an Austrian branch. The Spanish line died out in 1700 and the Austrians lost their Spanish claims. After the male line of the Habsburgs died out in 1740, the daughter of the late emperor Charles VI, Maria Theresa, became Austria's most famous empress. It was at this time that the Habsburg practice of gaining power through marriage rather than war was most challenged by other European powers. After the War of Austrian Succession, Maria Theresa's Austria had both gained and lost territory. (For more about Maria Theresa and the Habsburgs, see **Point 43, Imperial Germany and Austria**.) By the 19th century the Habsburg empire had been reduced to the Austro-Hungarian Dual Monarchy (1867), an empire that would also prove too unwieldy to last. Internal strife among the many peoples ruled by the Dual Monarchy helped lead to the outbreak of World War I. After the war, because there had been no official Habsburg abdication, Austria passed a law forbidding any member of the House of Habsburg from entering the country and claiming any royal rights (1919). As recently as 1961 the Austrian government refused the request of one of the last remaining Habsburgs, Archduke Otto, to return even as a private citizen.

38. HEALTH AND FITNESS

All of the German-speaking countries enjoy a high level of health care. Infant mortality rates are lower and life expectancy is higher than are those of the United States. The German health care system was taken as a model by the Clinton administration in its efforts to reform the U.S. system. While not without its problems, the Austrian and German government-sponsored **Krankenkasse** ("sickness fund") system helps provide universal coverage in Austria and Germany. Switzerland relies on private insurance, as does the U.S.

Most Europeans are accustomed to socialized, cradle-to-grave health care paid for by the employer, employee, and taxes. In Germany, the average employee salary contribution is about 13 percent (ranging from 8-16 percent). The unemployed, retirees, or those on welfare get government-paid coverage. Because of minimum income requirements, about half of the working population, mostly blue-collar workers, have no choice of which health plan they will join. The more affluent can opt out of the system, and private coverage is available for people who can afford to avoid the basic care of public facilities. A non-German resident will not be covered by the **Krankenkasse** unless qualifying through a German employer. Upon entering a hospital for treatment, a German presents a **Versicherungskarte** or insurance card. Payments to doctors, the hospital, or a health spa for in-patient or out-patient care go directly to the health care provider; the patient pays a modest share of only about 10 marks per day for a hospital visit.

A **Drogerie**, despite its name, doesn't sell drugs or medicines. A German "drug store" is more of a mini-mart for beauty products, toiletries, and detergents, but not medicines. The **Apotheke** is the German equivalent of a pharmacy. But you can't simply pick out a box of aspirin and pay for it. All the **Arzneimittel** or medications, prescription or not, are located behind the counter or in the back room.

Designated **Apotheken** stay open all night. To find out which one is open, any nearby **Apotheke** has a sign in the door indicating the one that is open that night. This information is also published in most German daily newspapers. The **Apotheker** can also help you avoid a trip to the doctor (**Arzt**) by giving you pharmacological advice. If you ask the pharmacist about a medical problem, he or she will usually be able to provide an appropriate ointment, pill, or salve. If you don't speak German, many pharmacists speak English. If you have a written prescription (**Rezept**) from a doctor, there is very little difficulty.

People in the German-speaking world are very health conscious. They are interested in prevention (**Vorbeugung**) as well as cure. Health foods, vitamins, natural foods, biologically-grown foods (**Biokost**), and herbal teas can be purchased at a **Reformhaus** or **Bioladen**. A **Kurort** is a resort for preventative medicine, recovery, or cure. It can be a spa (**Kurbad**) or a resort famed for its fresh air and climate (**Luftkurort**). Europeans, especially the German-speaking ones, hold "taking the waters" in high regard. A few days at a **Bad** (baht) or spa can do wonders for anyone's health, even if it's just to relax you. But various spas or **Bäder** (BAY-der) are known for waters that cure a specific health problem; certain spas have water with particular minerals that are claimed to be best for certain ailments. Taking the waters ("**eine Kur machen**") can involve drinking them, swimming in them, or both. Going to a spa or **Bad** is also covered by Austrian and German health insurance plans. A doctor may prescribe **eine Kur**.

Baden-Baden, Bad Homburg, Baden-Württemberg, Wiesbaden, Bad Dürkheim, and all the other German place names with some form of **Bad** derive their meaning from the Roman baths or spas that were once located there. Many, such as Baden-Baden, still attract visitors to their baths today. The word **Bad** in front of a German town's name is an official designation as a **Heil- und Kurbad**, a health and curative spa.

One area in which German Europe seems to be less health conscious than most of North America is smoking. For Germans over the age of 17, the smoking rate is a shocking 44 percent for males and 37 percent for females. Despite health warnings on cigarette packages and ads similar to those in the U.S., Austrians, Germans, and Swiss continue to light up more than Americans. Although one does see an occasional non-smoking area in restaurants, this practice is still rare. Germany's small anti-cigarette lobby continues to be outgunned by the tobacco interests, and more than 70 percent of Germans are opposed to legislation banning smoking in public places. Austrians and Swiss are similarly inclined. However, there was one small victory for the small anti-smoking lobby: in 1974 cigarette advertising was banned from German television.

German-speaking scientists and physicians have long been leaders in pioneering medical breakthroughs. The vital medical tool of x-rays was discovered by **Wilhelm Conrad Röntgen** (1845-1923) and the German word for x-ray is **Röntgen**. The Austrian physician **Leopold von Auenbrugg** (1722-1809) developed the diagnostic procedure of tapping a patient's chest or back (percussion) to determine the amount of fluid in the chest, a technique used to this day. **Robert Koch** (1843-1910) won a Nobel Prize in 1905 for his work on tuberculosis. He also made important discoveries related to anthrax, diphtheria, cholera, and other diseases. Austrian-American **Karl Landsteiner** (1868-1943) discovered the four primary blood types in 1901. He came to the U.S. in 1922 and received the Nobel Prize for medicine for his work in immunology und virus diseases. Aspirin was invented by a chemist with the German Bayer chemical firm in 1893. One of the most famous doctors of all time was born in German Alsace, now in France. **Albert Schweitzer** (1875-1965) spent most of his life in French Equatorial Africa caring for the native inhabitants. He received the Nobel Peace Prize in 1952.

39. HOLIDAYS AND CELEBRATIONS

Legal Holidays (*Feiertage*)

The legal holidays (**Feiertage**) on the calendar in the German-speaking world:

1. Januar New Year, **Neujahr**, is ushered in with fireworks and parties on New Year's Eve (**Silvester**).

6. Januar Epiphany, **Heilige drei Könige** (Three Kings) is observed in Austria, Baden-Württemberg and Bavaria in Germany, and in Catholic areas of Switzerland.

Karfreitag (Good Friday)

Ostersonntag (Easter Sunday)

Ostermontag (Easter Monday)

1. Mai Labor Day, **Tag der Arbeit**, is celebrated in most of Europe on this date.

Christi Himmelfahrt (Ascension Day) is observed in Catholic regions. Also **Vatertag** or **Herrentag** in all the German states.

Pfingstsonntag (Whitsunday) is also called Pentecost (**Pfingsten**) in English.

Pfingstmontag (Whitmonday)

71

Fronleichnam (Corpus Christi) In June. Not observed in the northern and eastern **Länder**.

1. August Swiss National Day is a time for fireworks, Alpine bonfires, lantern-lit nighttime parades, and the inevitable political speeches.

15. August Assumption of the Blessed Virgin, **Mariä Himmelfahrt**; in Catholic regions.

3. Oktober Day of German Unity, **Tag der deutschen Einheit**, commemorates the official date of German reunification in 1990. The date became a legal holiday in 1992.

26. Oktober Flag Day is the Austrian national holiday, celebrating the founding of the Republic of Austria on October 26, 1955.

Erntedankfest (Harvest Thanksgiving) is not a legal holiday, but many rural areas celebrate a bountiful harvest on the first Sunday in October with church services and other traditions. (Sorry, no turkey and cranberry sauce.) Switzerland observes the Federal Day of Prayers, a type of thanksgiving holiday, in mid-September.

31. Oktober Reformation Day, **Reformationstag**; only in Protestant areas.

1. November All Saints Day, **Allerheiligen**; observed in Austria and the Catholic regions of Germany and Switzerland.

Buß- und Bettag (Day of Repentance and Prayer); on a Wednesday in November; no longer a federal legal holiday since 1995.

6. Dezember St. Nicholas Day, **Nikolaustag** is when **Sankt Nikolaus** (not Santa Claus) brings small gifts to children. Similar to Christmas Day in the U.S., on the morning of Dec. 6, children wake up to find candy, cookies, and small presents brought by Sankt Nikolaus in their boots or shoes. (Not a legal holiday.)

24. Dezember Christmas Eve, **Heiligabend**, is the most important part of Christmas festivities in Germany, even though the legal holiday doesn't begin until the 25th. (However, stores and businesses close early on the 24th.) On this evening, presents are exchanged as the family gathers around the Christmas tree (**Tannenbaum, Weihnachtsbaum**, or **Christbaum**).

25.-26. Dezember Christmas Day, **Weihnachtstag**, and the following day (called Boxing Day in Britain) are legal holidays in Germany.

Other Significant Dates

These dates represent significant events in German history.

9. November is the anniversary of the opening of the Berlin Wall in 1989. Because it happens to also be the date of the infamous **Kristallnacht** night of terror against Jewish establishments during the Nazi period, the German parliament decided not to celebrate the date by making it an official holiday.

17. Juni Former **Tag der deutschen Einheit** (Day of German Unity); it commemorated the 1953 uprising in East Berlin and other cities of East Germany that was quickly squashed when Soviet tanks moved in. In honor of the day, the Berlin street running westward from the Brandenburg Gate is named **Straße des 17. Juni**. Following German reunification, Unity Day was changed to October 3.

Festivals

Maibaum (May tree) is a southern German, Austrian, and Swiss spring tradition involving the felling of a tall pine, a pole-raising ceremony, dancing, and partying.

Oktoberfest actually begins in the latter part of September and ends in October. This Munich holiday began long ago as a wedding celebration and has become the world's largest salute to beer.

Weinfeste (wine festivals) take place in various wine-growing regions. Hundreds of communities in Austria, Germany, and Switzerland celebrate their own **Weinfest** at different times from June to September.

11. November Karneval, Fasching, Fasnet, Fassenacht (Carnival, Mardi Gras) Although not a legal holiday, this is the traditional beginning of the carnival season in Catholic regions. Cities like Cologne, Mainz, and Munich in Germany, as well as all of Austria, and most of Switzerland practically shut down for the culmination of the Mardi Gras season on **Rosenmontag** (Rose Monday) and the Tuesday before **Aschermittwoch** (Ash Wednesday) when the festivities end for Lent. The foolishness begins officially at 11 past the 11th hour on the 11th day of the 11th month.

School Holidays and Vacation Periods

The dates of the various school holidays vary from country to country, and summer vacation periods are staggered, with some German **Bundesländer** getting out in mid-June and others in late July. Each year a vacation schedule for all of Germany is issued, and it varies from year to year. Generally, for summer, the northern **Länder** get out early, and the southern **Länder** get out later in the summer. Vacation periods in Austria and Switzerland are similar. The following school vacation periods are standard except as noted: Autumn (in Sept., Oct., or Nov.), Christmas, Winter (in Feb. in Austria, Berlin and the five eastern states of Germany), Easter, Spring (Hamburg only; doesn't include Easter), **Pfingsten** (Pentecost/Whitsun; in May/June; not in Saarland or Schleswig-Holstein), Summer (six weeks).

40. HOUSE AND HOME

Schöner Wohnen ("living more beautifully") is a popular German house and garden magazine. Like Americans, most Germans dream of living in their own house with a beautiful lawn and garden. "*Schaffe, schaffe, Häusle baue,*" ("Work, work, build your little house.") goes the old Swabian saying. However, Germans find this dream more difficult to fulfill than Americans. A house in Germany, Austria, or Switzerland is a very expensive dream. The average cost of land and construction is double or triple that in the United States. Add to this a much larger down payment of between 30 and 50 percent, and you can see why most Germans live in apartments or condominiums. Only 39 percent of Germans own their own home, compared to 64 percent in the U.S. and 68 percent in the U.K. Those Germans who do finally realize the dream of their own house are often in their forties or fifties when it happens.

In or around almost any German city, you will see the rows of **Wohnsilos** (residential towers), the tall and usually Spartan-looking apartment towers that dominate the cityscape, and were mostly constructed in the last ten years to provide the higher quality housing that Germans expect today. Lacking the charm of traditional European architecture, these utilitarian living units most often resemble the unexciting condos and apartments that can be found all over Europe and the world. Built in response to a chronic lack of housing, these towers are usually located in what are termed "satellite towns" at the edges of the city.

Even renting can be expensive unless you are lucky enough to live in an apartment complex subject to rent control. In the private sector, rents can be sky high, especially as the process of "yuppie gentrification," which began about ten or fifteen years ago, continues all over German-speaking Europe. This gentrification includes the process of tearing down older housing or of renovating older buildings to make way for more prosperous residents. Sleepy, small towns on the outskirts of cities are becoming up-scale bedroom communities that are just a short drive from the residents' place of work. In reaction to this phenomenon, which makes less low-cost housing available for low-income people and drives original residents out of the area, there have been a growing number of protests of various kinds. These protests have ranged from signs in apartment windows ("Wir bleiben hier!"—We're staying here!) to demonstrations in the streets. The protests, in whatever form, are directed at real estate speculators and at government officials who, in the eyes of the protesters, are driving up the cost of housing.

That Austrian, German, and Swiss houses and apartment complexes often all seem to have been poured from the same mold is no accident. Communities (**Gemeinden**) have strict codes and covenants regarding not only how a house must be constructed, but also how it must look. Laws and regulations prescribe requirements right down to such details as what color and of what material the roof has to be.

(This is similar to the "codes, covenants, and restrictions" on house color and roofing materials found in exclusive housing developments in the U.S.) This gives European towns and developments a certain harmony and uniformity that critics call monotonous. But it also avoids architectural clutter and lack of esthetic harmony.

Although the U.S. has its share of cookie-cutter "little boxes all in a row" housing, it rarely has the degree of design control, for good or bad, that one sees in Europe. It is a reflection, once again, of Germanic "social contract" thinking, in which the common good justifies curtailing certain personal freedoms. This control leads to the experience of looking out over a town and seeing a harmonious scene dominated by red tile roofs and well-tended yards.

Inside a German, Austrian, or Swiss home, the architecture reflects the teutonic love of compartmentalization and privacy. The open architecture favored in North American homes is rare; thick walls and solid doors define borders between rooms, and the doors are usually closed. The thick (usually masonry) walls give a sense of permanency and stability, reflecting the European belief that a home should be built to last for generations. Even the living room (**Wohnzimmer**) and dining room (**Eßzimmer**) are usually entered through a door. Newer homes often have a so-called "American" bathroom, but in older homes the **Toilette** and the **Bad** (bath) are separate rooms. Homes built in the last twenty years or so often acknowledge the Germanic love of nature and the outdoors by providing a large sliding glass door that opens onto a patio (**Terrasse**) and the back yard and garden. Inevitably, there will be a large retractable awning over the patio. Even the tiniest newer apartments provide at least glass-door access to a balcony (**Balkon**).

A German bedroom (**Schlafzimmer**) is not really unlike an American one, but there are a few interesting differences. German beds tend to be both narrower and shorter than the U.S. variety. Anyone who is around six feet tall or better will usually feel a bit cramped in a German bed. While there are exceptions, it is rare to see a genuine double bed, even in the master bedroom. What at first glance seems to be a double bed is actually two single beds set side-by-side. There is a dividing line down the middle where the two bed sections have been joined. Although there is sometimes a double-width comforter over them, there are two separate mattresses underneath. Often there are also two separate comforters.

German **Bettzeug** (BET-tsoyk) or bedding is also a bit different from what an American is used to. Instead of sheets and blankets, Germans sleep under a **Federbett**, or down comforter that lies atop a mattress covered with a fabric that is often more like terry cloth than a linen sheet. On cold nights, the German **Federbett** is ideal—very cozy and snug. But in the summer, on warm nights, the down comforter is too warm, and your choice is either to sleep without any cover or to sweat under the **Federbett**. If you want a top sheet or light blanket, you usually have to get your own. Fortunately, the German climate is generally on the cool side, so most of the time the **Federbett** is a good idea. Traditionally, the **Federbett** was hung out over a windowsill or a balcony rail each morning to air. You will still often see white **Bettzeug** hanging from German apartment windows in the morning hours.

Although some newer homes have built-in closets, it is more common to see a **Kleiderschrank** (KLY-der-schrahnk), a free-standing wood cabinet with doors that serves as a closet. A **Kleiderschrank** may be sleekly modern or rustically traditional in design, depending on its owner's tastes.

41. HUMOR

Germans, Austrians, and the Swiss have an undeserved reputation for being humorless. The old joke about the world's shortest book being "One Thousand Years of German Humor" is an unfair stereotype. While they may not be as outgoing or as fun-loving as Italians or Spaniards, there actually is such a thing as a Germanic sense of humor. The lazy, sausage-nosed "Werner," a popular cartoon character drawn by Rötger Feldmann, has appeared in more than 3.5 million comics. Berliners are known for their "**Berliner Schnauze**" or Berlin wit. German humor often takes the form of satire. German-speaking university students today enjoy the posters, comics, and irreverent comments of "**das kleine Arschloch**," a cartoon character whose name and actions are the somewhat stronger German equivalent of the Butt-Head character in the "Beavis and Butt-Head" duo. Since the 1920s Berlin cabaret has been drawing audiences with its political satire. *Mad* magazine's German edition has long been popular. The German satirical magazine *Simplicissimus* was published from 1896 to 1944 and again from 1954 to 1967. Today Berlin's irreverent *Titanic* magazine carries on the tradition of political and cultural satire. In the 1930s the Bavarian vaudeville comic Karl Valentin's bittersweet, illogical humor enlivened Munich cabarets and a few films. Because his Bavarian dialect and sense of humor were difficult even for other Germans to understand, his fame was limited even in Germany.

Wilhelm Busch invented the comic strip in 1865 with *Max und Moritz*, later to be Americanized as the Katzenjammer Kids. In the last few years German filmmakers have managed to lure the home audience into cinemas with a spate of successful comedies—one of the few inroads made into Hollywood's dominance of the German film market.

The German language has many interesting and humorous turns of phrase; many reflect a certain Germanic wry wit. Berliners in particular are known for their penchant of giving almost everything in their city a nickname: the gutted Kaiser Wilhelm Memorial Church with its broken church tower is known as "**der hohle Zahn**" ("the hollow tooth"); the modernistic *Kongresshalle* with its parabolic roof does actually resemble a "**schwangere Auster**" or "pregnant oyster." Germany being greener than the old West may help explain why "to bite the dust" is "**ins Gras beissen**" or "to bite into the grass." There are several other interesting "grass" expressions in German. "**Das Gras wachsen hören**" means to "hear the grass grow" or, in other words, to think you're so clever that you can even hear the grass grow. "**Über etwas Gras wachsen lassen**" ("to let grass grow over something") means to leave something in the past, to allow something to be forgotten. Other expressions make use of different mental images for their effect. When a German has had just a little bit too much to drink, "**er hat zu tief ins Glas geguckt**" ("he looked too deeply into the glass"). To fill up the glass again is "**die Luft aus dem Glas 'rauslassen**," to "let the air out of the glass." Another **Luft** expression is "**gesiebte Luft atmen**," which literally means to "breathe strained air," a slang expression meaning to be in jail and breathing air filtered through the bars of your cell.

42. THE IDENTITY CARD (*der Ausweis*) AND OTHER RED TAPE

The standard German ID card, known as the **Personalausweis**, is used like a U.S. drivers license. German-speakers, accustomed to a level of official registration and supervision that Americans find rather Orwellian, carry this card as a handy mini-passport. In fact, the **Personalausweis** functions as a sort of passport for Germans and Austrians traveling within the European Union, where they do not need a regular passport.

But even if a German-speaker just wants to move from one apartment to another in the same building, he must register his new address with the authorities. This **Anmeldung** is required within a few days of moving, whether within a building or across the country. If you move away, then **Abmeldung** (deregistration) is necessary before you leave. To take care of **Anmeldung** or **Abmeldung**, contact the registration office (**Einwohnermeldeamt**) at the city hall (**Rathaus**) or, in larger cities, the nearest police station (**Polizeirevier, Polizeiwache**, or **Gendarmerie**).

43. IMPERIAL GERMANY AND AUSTRIA

Most Germans today are unaware of Germany's former imperial efforts. Unlike those of rivals England or France, Germany's former colonies proved to be short-lived and rather insignificant in the long run. During its "Imperial" period, roughly 1871-1918 (up to 1890 under Otto von Bismarck), Prussia established colonial outposts that extended the German Reich's influence as far as Africa and the South Pacific. Germany's loss of World War I put an end to its 19th century "empire." Unlike the British and French African colonies that provided a degree of raw materials, power and influence, German efforts in Africa were slow to produce any tangible benefits. As a result, Bismarck soon lost interest in his expansionist adventures, but it was too late to go against pro-colony, pro-expansion attitudes at home. Bismarck was stuck with his far-flung colonies, even though they were more of a burden than an asset. His successors took Bismarck's reluctant imperialism, combined it with Prussian arrogance, and finally managed to start the world's first world war.

The "German" South Pacific

The Prussian flag was first hoisted in New Guinea on Nov. 16, 1884. German commercial interests had been growing in the South Pacific since about 1857. By 1880 the Deutsche Seehandelgesellschaft (German Sea Trading Co.) in Berlin had been founded; its interests in New Guinea and the South Pacific prompted the British to pay closer attention to the area. When, in 1884, Bismarck promised protection to German trading interests in the Pacific, Britain established a "temporary protectorate" over New Guinea. Bismarck met that challenge by annexing a part of the mainland and naming it **Kaiserwilhelmsland**. But the Neu-Guinea Kompanie, granted an imperial charter in 1885, never achieved much success; the German government had to take over control in 1899. Right at the outbreak of the First World War in August 1914, Australian troops ended the German adventure in New Guinea by marching into **Kaiserwilhelmsland**.

Cameroon

Bismarck and Prussia did not have any better luck in Africa. Cameroon (**Kamerun**) was a German protectorate between 1884 and 1919. Because the British showed little interest, even after Bismarck told them he was going to move in, Germany acquired parts of the African east coast that had not previously been claimed by other European nations. The British and the French made only feeble efforts to challenge the Prussian takeover, and the Germans somewhat reluctantly established a presence in **Kamerun** that ended at the conclusion of World War I. Cameroon became a UN mandate and in 1960 the British and French Cameroons were united to form an independent Cameroon.

Rwanda

The German presence in Ruanda-Urundi (today Rwanda and Burundi) was hardly that. This area of East Africa came under Prussian control in 1890, but the 24-year German occupation amounted to just a solitary military camp on the shores of Lake Tanganyika. The territory came under Belgian control during World War I.

Namibia

Probably the most successful 19th century German colony was German South West Africa, today the independent nation of Namibia. German influence in South West Africa began in 1840 with the arrival of German missionaries. Later tribal wars prompted the missionaries to ask the British for protection both in 1868 and 1880, but the British refused. The first German farmers settled near Windhoek, the territory's new capital, in 1892. Fighting and disputes with the native peoples marred the German presence in the region up until 1907, but the discovery of diamonds near Lüderitz Bay in 1908 helped bring the European population to almost 15,000 by 1913. World War I forced Germany to give up its South West Africa colony along with all its other colonies; the German settlers were allowed to return home to Germany after the war.

On March 21, 1990, the former territory became the independent country of Namibia. The 83,000 white minority in Namibia (mainly of German and Dutch heritage) today enjoys generally good relations with the country's majority black population (about 1.5 million). Namibia's progressive government, ruling from the tidy capital of Windhoek (pop. 150,000), has created an exceptional democracy in a region known more for conflict and dictatorships. Despite the communist guerrilla background of the Swapo governing party, Namibians read a free press, and talk shows openly criticize the government. Namibia, a country twice the size of California, does have some problems. A high unemployment rate, unstable neighbors in Angola, and white domination of business and farming are just a few. But the country has natural resources in minerals, diamonds, ranching, fish, and wildlife.

Tsingtao (Qingdao)

Along with several other world powers, the Germans joined in the colonization of parts of China. But German efforts would prove far less successful than British Hong Kong or Portuguese Macao. From 1898 to 1914, the port of Tsingtao, today's Qingdao with almost two million inhabitants, was the principal city of the Jiaozhou territory, a German colony located on the shores of Jiaozhou Bay on the Yellow Sea. In 1898 the Germans were granted a 99-year lease to the territory. Although a Japanese invasion drove the Germans out in 1914, German architecture from the colonial expansion of Qingdao dominates the city to this day, and Chinese beers trace their origin back to German brewers a century ago.

The Austrian Empire

The 600 years of Habsburg rule in Austria and Europe (Spain, Italy, Netherlands) were made possible in part by the royal family's policy of politically advantageous marriages. Thus the saying, "**Andere Länder führen Kriege, du glückliches Österreich heirate.**" ("Other lands wage war; you, happy Austria, marry.") It was during the rule of the Habsburg Empress Maria Theresa (1717-1780) that Haydn and Mozart composed many of their great musical works in imperial Vienna. Maria Theresa introduced many reforms and proved to be a wise ruler of the empire. Austria and Vienna suffered at the hands of Napoleon, but the Austrian Prince Metternich (1773-1859) presided over the 1815 Congress of Vienna that restored the old order until Metternich too was swept away in the revolutions of 1848.

In 1867 Hungary achieved equal rights in the Austro-Hungarian dual monarchy. During this peaceful time, prior to World War I, Vienna and Austria prospered and moved into the modern age. Even today Kaiser (Emperor) Franz Joseph (1830-1916) remains a symbol of Austria's later imperial past. (It was Franz Joseph's brother Maximilian, as emperor of Mexico, who was executed in 1867 on the orders of Benito Juarez.) The 1914 assassination of the heir to the Austrian throne, Archduke Ferdinand, in Sarajevo sparked the beginning of the first world war and the end of the Austrian empire.

44. THE KITCHEN (die Küche)

The **Küche** or kitchen in a German, Austrian, or Swiss home is usually smaller and more compact than its U.S. counterpart—not only because European homes and apartments themselves tend to be smaller, but also because European kitchen appliances are smaller and more economical. A typical refrigerator (**Kühlschrank**) is about half the size of an American one. It therefore holds about half as much and uses half the energy. Full size refrigerators are also available for those who prefer them and have the money to pay for the extra electricity.

German kitchens are set up pretty much the same as American kitchens. The range (**Herd**) and oven (**Backofen**) may be either gas or electric. Although it has been slower to catch on with the European **Hausfrau**, microwave oven (**Mikrowellenofen**) use is increasing. Automatic dish washers (**Geschirrspülmaschinen**) can be found in more and more German households. Much more rare, in fact almost non-existent in German kitchens, is the in-sink garbage disposal.

In some older houses and apartments (and in many homes in former East Germany) there may be a special miniature gas hot water heater mounted on the wall over the kitchen sink. Although this European phenomenon is fading from the kitchen scene in Germany, it was popular for so long because it saved money on utility bills by quickly heating just enough water to do the dishes or to take a bath. As soon as the hot water is turned off, the heater turns off. Most modern homes and apartments now have a larger central water heater.

If you are planning to buy or rent a German apartment, be aware that it usually comes with a "bare" kitchen. "Bare" is indeed the right word. Your new kitchen may be nothing more than four bare walls with roughed-in plumbing and electrical connections—even the kitchen sink may be missing!

The German word **Küche** also means cooking or cuisine. **Deutsche Küche** means German cuisine.

45. LANGUAGE

All educated speakers of German learn **Hochdeutsch** (high German). Newspaper and other publications, be they in Austria, Switzerland, or Germany, are generally printed in **Hochdeutsch**, the *lingua franca* of the German world. If a Bavarian from Munich wants to communicate with a "Prussian" from Hamburg, they would have a very difficult time understanding each other's local dialects. The problem is solved by **Hochdeutsch**, standard German, a language common to both speakers.

German was historically slow to develop into a standard language. The German language has been as fragmented as German history itself. Martin Luther and his German translation of the Bible (New Testament, 1522; Old Testament, 1534), though not the first, became one of the most important steps toward a unified German orthography and grammar, primarily because of the impact of the printing press. Luther's stylistic treatment and his linguistic borrowings (primarily from Saxony) proved to be so successful that the **Lutherbibel** came to be a standard, even for biblical translations in other languages.

Written German (**Schriftsprache**), thanks to Luther and the growth of both printing and trade, became more or less standardized by around 1650. But it would take another two centuries before significant works on German grammar and spelling would appear. First the Grimm brothers (1854) and then Konrad Duden (1880) published extensive German dictionaries. Duden's *Vollständiges orthographisches Wörterbuch der deutschen Sprache* became the Webster's of the German language; even today the Duden name is still associated with "proper" German.

With today's greater influence of radio, television, and the movies, drastic differences in dialect are not as common as they once were. But a visitor staying in Bavaria, Austria, or German Switzerland would not be as likely to hear as standardized a version of German as would generally be the case in central Germany. Even the "standard German"—also called **Bühnendeutsch**, "stage German"—heard on Austrian or Swiss radio or television has a definite charming Austrian/Swiss lilt that a German can detect immediately. To put it in an English perspective, it is somewhat similar to the difference between an American and a British accent. The Munich/Hamburg difference in dialect could be compared to Atlanta/Boston, although an Atlantan and a Bostonian would be more likely to understand each other than would a **Münchner** and a **Hamburger**. (Yes, a person from Hamburg is called a **Hamburger**, masc. or a **Hamburgerin**, fem.)

Germany's new unity has brought to light yet another language division: the east-west split. In only 40 years, the two parts of Germany managed to develop their own linguistic divide. What a western German calls a "**Supermarkt**" is called a "**Kaufhalle**" by eastern Germans. Various cultural and historical factors combined to create different vocabularies on each side of the inner-German border. On the eastern side, regional dialects have remained much more entrenched than in western Germany—the result of communist Germany's isolation and its less open, less mobile society. (See also **Point 20, Dialects**)

46. LEISURE AND VACATIONS

Among all the nations of the world, few nationalities have more **Wanderlust** than the Germans, nor more vacation time to carry out their desire to travel. The Germanic love of travel and nature has a long tradition. The German Alpine Society was founded in 1869; today its success is also a problem. The Alps (in all three German-speaking lands) have become an environmental disaster caused by too many tourists and Alpine climbers. More than almost any other culture, the German-speakers have a love of hiking and **die Natur**. No doubt in response to urban living, and the relatively high degree of urbanization, there is a compulsion to get out "into the green" of nature (**ins Grüne**), to climb mountains and hills, and hike through the woods. The German Leisure Association was formed in 1971 to conduct research into leisure time behavior and to provide information. Germany has 300,000 clubs and associations for every interest—sports, chess, gardening, dog breeding, choirs, amateur radio, etc.

There is perhaps no more revered German custom today than **Urlaub** or vacation. Despite, or perhaps because of, a strong work ethic, Austrians, Germans, and the Swiss believe in taking time off for work well done. The Germans in particular rank among the world's most traveled people. This traditional travel fever dates back to Goethe and his *Italienische Reise* (*Italian Journey*) of 1786-87, and certainly to one of the greatest travelers and adventurers of all time (and an acquaintance of Goethe), Alexander von Humboldt from Berlin. In 1799 the well-to-do Humboldt traveled to South America, where he cataloged some 60,000 species of plants. He later lived in Paris and, in 1829, ventured off to Russia and Siberia for more scientific inquiries.

Since reunification, the eastern Germans, making up for lost time and opportunity with a vengeance, have shown that the love of vacation and travel is a pan-German phenomenon. The easterners left their homes for a vacation of five days or more at a rate even greater than the western German 70 percent. Germans may be known as hard workers, but German industrial employees receive an average of 30 paid vacation days per year. (The average for the United States is only 12 days.) Most of Europe averages between 21 and 27 vacation days. Only workers in Italy (32 days), the Netherlands (32.5) and Finland (37.5) get more time off than the Germans do.

Contemporary German travelers may not be quite as ambitious as Humboldt or have as much time, but the most popular foreign vacation destinations today include Goethe's favorite, Italy, as well as Spain, Austria, France, Switzerland, and the United States (which Humboldt also visited briefly). Germans love sailing among the Greek isles, sunbathing in the Bahamas or the Canaries, and generally seeking out the sun that so often eludes them in their native land. When they desire cooler climes, Germans also venture northward to the fresh green coolness of Scandinavia. With increased access to eastern Europe—where the D-mark, Austrian schilling, or Swiss franc also goes further—Poland, Hungary, former Czechoslovakia, and even Russia have become increasingly popular. If they don't want to go abroad, Germans have their own country half the size of Texas to explore. Closer to home and not nearly as expensive as Euro Disneyland near Paris, the German **Europa-Park** in Rust in southwest Germany opened in 1975. Its rides and attractions have a European theme such as rafting along a "Norwegian" fjord. The "Medieval Knights' Feast" takes place in a real castle dating back to 1442.

Every summer, as soon as school is out, the Germans, Austrians, and Swiss clog the highways in a mad dash to get away. Others climb aboard charter flights to visit Turkey, Spain, or some other sunny spot. In any case, it is difficult to find a German at home in the summer.

47. MARRIAGE AND DIVORCE

As in some other parts of Europe, a ring on the left hand signifies an engagement in the German-speaking lands. The wedding ring is worn on the right hand. In Austria, Germany, and Switzerland—countries with no official separation of church and state—a marriage, to be legal, must be performed by the state at the **Standesamt** or marriage bureau, usually located in the city hall (**Rathaus**). The church wedding or **Hochzeit** following the brief civil ceremony is a strictly optional, but still popular, tradition. Instead of tin cans tied to the rear of the car, the wedding couple's car outside the **Standesamt** can be recognized by the flowers and ribbons decorating the hood.

Considering the image of the proper, upstanding German citizen, it is surprising to learn that in former East Germany, marriage is so unpopular that 42 percent of all children are born illegitimately (12 percent in former West Germany), although most are born into a two-parent family and are raised by their unmarried mother and father. The marriage rate per 1000 is 5.6 in Austria and 6.7 in Germany. (The U.S. rate is 9.2 per 1000.)

Polterabend is a noisy custom preceding the wedding day. Probably related to the old German saying "**Scherben bringen Glück**," or "broken glass (or pottery) brings good luck," the tradition calls for friends of the couple to go to the bride's house and smash up old plates, pottery or dinnerware just outside the door. To help ensure a happy marriage, the bride sweeps up the broken pieces herself.

Should things not work out so happily, legislation in 1957 gave German women equal rights concerning joint property in a marriage, but still limited a wife's right to work if her husband did not approve! Since 1977 German women and men have been able to obtain a divorce without proving the guilt of the other party, and a divorcee is entitled to full pension benefits. Austria now has similar laws. About a third of all German married couples end up in divorce court. But this divorce rate is still lower than that of the U.S.; Germany's divorce rate is about half that in America, where almost 50 percent of marriages end in divorce.

48. THE MILITARY

The German army has a long and rather dark history. Today's **Bundeswehr** (federal defense force), however, is nothing like the **Wehrmacht** of the Nazi era, or even the Prussian imperial army of old. In fact, critics often make an issue of the fact that the present German army, by constitutional constraint, may not be deployed outside of Germany. It took a long legal battle just to establish the recent right to send German troops on UN and NATO peacekeeping missions, and that decision by the German Constitutional Court was not without controversy in Germany.

All German 18-year-old males are required to serve either 10 months in the armed forces or, for conscientious objectors, 13 months of public service, usually in a hospital or senior citizens home. In recent years, more and more men are choosing the public service option, prompting concerns about adequate staffing for Germany's armed forces. Women are allowed to serve only in the medical and music corps.

During the 40 years of German division there were two German armies. The former **Nationale Volksarmee** (NVA) of the German Democratic Republic was disbanded at the time of German reunification in 1990, and merged with the western **Bundeswehr**. At the same time, plans were made to reduce the size of the **Bundeswehr** (army, navy and air force). NATO forces stationed in Germany by the U.S., Canada, and other nations, as well as Russia's Warsaw Pact troops in former East Germany are also being reduced or withdrawn, both as a result of the end of Cold War tensions and united Germany's regained sovereignty. The Federal Republic of Germany has been a member of NATO since 1955, and it continues to provide the largest single contingent of NATO troops in Europe. But one sign of the ambivalent attitude about the armed forces in Germany is this graffito, spray-painted on a building in Germany: ''To be or NATO be.'' For some Germans, that is the question.

The Swiss citizen-army is unique in several striking ways. First of all, unlike all other modern armed forces in the world, the Swiss army has no commander-in-chief, no head general except in time of war. In the event of actual hostilities, a commanding general is elected by parliament, as happened during both world wars. (Besides reflecting Switzerland's vaunted neutrality, this is also the military equivalent of the ''primus inter pares'' [''**Erster unter Gleichen**,'' ''first among equals''] principle, under which Switzerland's federal president, **Bundespräsident**, is merely the head of parliament and the official Swiss representative abroad, but not the head of state.) Except for a basic corps of 500 military instructors, the Swiss army maintains no standing army or permanent forces. Military service is required of all males between 20 and 50 (55 for officers). Men judged unfit must pay a special military tax in lieu of service. Swiss women may volunteer for service in the **Militärischer Frauendienst** (MFD). After basic training, Swiss militiamen undergo several annual training exercises, the number and length of which depend on age and rank. Each citizen soldier is required to keep his uniform and weapon at home, ready at any time for rapid mobilization. During peacetime the army is run by a National Defense Committee. The Department of Defense (**Eidgenössisches Militärdepartement**) is housed in the Swiss capital of Bern.

In Austria the armed forces follow a pattern similar to the German model. All 18-year old Austrian males must serve a compulsory six-month tour of duty in the Austrian **Bundesheer** (federal army), with two more months of reserve duty at various times after that. Conscientious objectors must do some sort of public service. There are three corps of the Austrian army plus an air corps unit based near Vienna. Austrian troops have taken part in several UN missions around the world since 1960.

49. MONEY, BANKS, AND CREDIT

Germany has a vital banking tradition that dates back to the great Fugger money-lending empire in the 15th and 16th centuries, and before that, the limited banking practices required by the Hanseatic League (**Hansa**) of northern Germany in the 14th century. Germany's first commercial bank was established in Hamburg in 1619. The **Giro** bank lasted until its takeover by the state-run Reichsbank in 1875.

By the early 1800s Frankfurt am Main was a banking center under the House of Rothschild. The Rothschilds, in fact, took their name from the red (**roth**) shield (**Schild**) on the front of their Frankfurt home during the first years of the Jewish family's history. Their banking dynasty soon extended beyond Frankfurt to London, Naples, Paris, and Vienna. Between 1870 and 1872 several other important German banks evolved, some of which are still around in one form or another.

The five largest German banks are Deutsche Bank, Dresdner Bank, Bayerische Vereinsbank, Commerzbank, and the Bayerische Hypotheken- und Wechsel-Bank, known more affectionately as the Hypo-Bank. Only the Deutsche Bank ranks among the top 10 world banks in size (most are Japanese). Frankfurt's present-day skyline consists largely of the gleaming towers that serve as headquarters for

Germany's banks, a sight that has led to one of the German financial capital's nicknames: "Bankfurt." Frankfurt also won the heated contest to house the European Monetary Institute (EMI), a precursor of the proposed European Central Bank. The EMI began operations in Frankfurt in January 1994. Now more than ever, Germany can rightfully bill itself as **Finanzplatz Deutschland**—Germany, the Financial Center. Germany's **Bundesbank**, known as the Buba to the financially literate, is Europe's most influential central bank, controlling the ups and downs of Europe's currencies with its strict interest rates and its control over the mighty deutschmark. For all practical purposes, the Bundesbank is to Europe what the U.S. Federal Reserve Bank is to the U.S.

Commercial banks in Germany are usually engaged in a much broader range of activities than banks in the U.S. In fact, much of what German banks do would be illegal in American banking. German banks sell securities, lease property, and conduct business in many other areas that would be **verboten** in America. German bankers sit on the boards of other industries, in a cozy interwoven relationship between banking and industry that is unheard of in the U.S. The Germans regard these strong ties between banking and business as an advantage that helps German companies to better survive economic ups and downs, and to be more independent of stockholder influence and the predatory raiding of companies that was so prevalent in the U.S. in the 1980s. (This again reflects the "social good" philosophy that pervades the German economy in general.)

Switzerland and banking are, of course, synonymous terms, with Zurich being the Swiss (and a world) financial center. Switzerland has nearly 600 banking institutions with many more branches and more than 1,100 savings banks (**Sparkassen**). In Austria the Creditanstalt bank and Bank Austria in the banking center of Vienna are two of the most important of the 1,100 financial institutions with 4,600 branches.

Most people are more concerned about which bank is closest and offers the best rates and services than about financial philosophy. Banking in Germany is divided into three types of institutions: the larger private commercial banks, like those mentioned previously, the savings banks (**Sparkassen**), and the cooperatives or credit unions (**Raiffeisenbanken, Volksbanken**). But German banking has been going through changes since reunification, particularly in the eastern part of the country, with mergers and blendings of banking types that may change the German banking landscape considerably.

In the United States people don't think of the post office when they think of banking, but the **Deutsche Post AG** (German Postal Service) offers certain banking services at any larger post office anywhere in Germany through its **Postbank**, Germany's 14th largest bank. A Post Office Saving Bank can't make loans or sell securities, but it does offer checking and savings accounts with the convenience of being able to use such services all over Germany and (through foreign postal services) across Europe. You will notice **Postsparkonto** signs in most German post offices. That's where you can deposit or withdraw savings in your postal savings account. With a **Postbank** card you can also withdraw cash from machines at most post offices.

When you enter a German, Austrian, or Swiss bank, it looks pretty much like a bank in America, but there are a few differences—only some of which have to do with the language. **Geldwechsel** (money exchange), **Girokonto/Sparkonto** (checking/savings account), and **Kasse** (cashier's window, teller) are the most important words to know. Many German banks, in characteristic German compartmentalization, only allow you to do certain things at certain windows. So watch for those signs. There is, however, a newer tendency for banks to be less specialized by window, and to offer a variety of services, American style, at most teller windows.

One thing most banks still have is the "glass cage." Whether you are cashing a traveler's check or withdrawing funds, you usually have to go to a special cashier's window, enclosed in thick bullet-proof glass, to collect your money. Although German banks usually have an open, relaxed interior decor, the glass cage is a reminder that Germany too has bank robbers.

Walk by any small-town bank in the most remote corner of Europe, and you will see the latest exchange rates for a multitude of national currencies on display (usually with colorful national flag symbols). Unless there is a special **Geldwechsel** window, any teller can quickly calculate the exchange on the bank computer, and you'll have your francs, marks, lire, pounds, or dollars in no time. Some banks and money exchanges ask to see your passport, while others don't. It's a good idea to carry your passport or other ID just in case. Often the ID check depends on whether you are exchanging cash or traveler's checks. You'll get a slightly better exchange rate for traveler's checks than for cash.

Germans have a checking account system that Americans find a little confusing. In the U.S. the personal checking account is used for paying bills, buying goods and services, and checks are made payable to an individual or a company name. The Germans do it differently; they use a **Geldüberweisung** or money transfer made out to an account number rather than a name. To pay for a magazine subscription, for example, you make out a transfer check (**Überweisung**) payable not to the magazine but to a **BLZ** and **Girokonto** number. A **BLZ** is a **Bankleitzahl** or bank code number, similar to the bank numbers you see on U.S. bank checks. A **Girokonto** (ZHEE-ro KON-toh) is a specific transfer account for a firm, organization, or person. (The number of the magazine's account would be printed on the order form for the magazine.) The **Überweisung** authorizes the bank to transfer a sum of money from your account to the magazine's account (like a check), but you have to do it by the numbers, and instead of sending a check to the magazine, you send (or take) the **Überweisung** to your bank.

Eurocheques are accepted all over Europe by stores, businesses, hotels and restaurants. Eurocheques are used in connection with the EC Card, a type of check guarantee card. You can obtain a Eurocheque account through a European bank, once you have established a good credit record. The bank can also provide automatic payment or electronic transfers for monthly or other regular billings. Almost any banking service you would expect in the U.S., plus some not offered in the U.S., is available from a European bank. If you have a computer and a modem, home banking is also available in Germany through Btx/T-Online, a German electronic service. Dozens of automatic teller machine (**Geldautomat**) networks are run by

Germany's banks. Keep in mind that there is usually a difference between Visa and MasterCard banks in Europe. An individual bank usually does not handle both Visa and MasterCard. Eurocard is the MasterCard equivalent in Germany. The increasing use of ATMs in German Europe means you can use your debit or credit card (Visa, MasterCard, American Express, etc.) to get cash conveniently almost anywhere. This is usually cheaper and easier than cashing traveler's checks, and you don't have to wait for the banks to open. Just pay attention to any possible extra fees and don't forget your PIN.

50. MOVIES: THE HOLLYWOOD FACTOR

Thanks to the former East Germans, Germans recently overtook the French as the most enthusiastic moviegoers in Europe; but less than 15 percent of the films they watch are from Germany. Over the last few decades, Europe has seen a steady decline in its movie production, while Hollywood has steadily increased its share of the European film market. In fact, most of the movies seen in Austria, Germany, and Switzerland today are Hollywood productions. Unlike the French, who have been pushing for a European quota system to limit the number of Hollywood films and U.S. TV programs shown in Europe, the Germans, Austrians, and Swiss seem to have accepted the American entertainment invasion, if not always without complaint. (Too much violence is one of the main ones.) Step into any video store (**Videothek**) in German-speaking Europe and you will see row after row of Hollywood films on display but very few original German-language productions. (See also **Point 14, Cinema**)

51. MUSEUMS

German-speaking lands are rich in museums and exhibitions. The great scope and variety of the many museums in Austria, Germany, and Switzerland would require several lifetimes and hundreds of sets of shoes to cover thoroughly. From the clock museum in Triberg (Black Forest) to the better-known **Deutsches Museum** of science and technology in Munich, from outdoor museums to small one-room exhibits, the range of museums is impressive. Switzerland's 600 or so museums not only include the traditional important art galleries in Basel, Geneva, and Zurich, but also less traditional displays such as the popular Swiss Transport Museum in Lucerne. All three countries have fascinating open-air museums (**Freilichtmuseen**) where vanishing forms of rural architecture are preserved and arranged in a natural setting. Austria's best-known is the **Österreichisches Freilichtmuseum** near Graz. Switzerland has its equivalent straddling the Ballenberg hillsides near Brienz. Germany has several open-air museums, with one of the best, the Vogtsbauernhof, located in the Black Forest not too far from Freiburg.

Illustrating the value that Germans place on their museums, the World War II-damaged Semper Gallery in Dresden celebrated its grand reopening in December 1992 in a building that is itself a renowned example of architecture. The Semper lays claim to about 700 paintings by Italian, Dutch, and German masters. The gallery was restored in a $60 million project that undid the neglect by communist East Germany in the years since its first restoration in the 1950s. The Semper Gallery's renowned collections of paintings by Dürer, Raphael, Rembrandt, Rubens, Titian, and other great painters was assembled by the kings of Saxony in the 18th century. Other extensive art collections are housed in museums in every major German-speaking city, most notably in Vienna, Munich, Zurich, Basel, and Berlin.

Berlin alone is home to more than 100 museums, four of which sit on the city's famous **Museuminsel** (Museum Island) in former East Berlin. One of the most notable there is the **Pergamon** with its huge Greek Pergamon Altar and the Ishtar Gate from the hanging gardens of Babylon. Other Berlin museums are largely concentrated in three other sections of Berlin: Dahlem, Tiergarten, and Charlottenburg. Berlin has two Egyptian museums, with Queen Nefertiti's classic bust residing in the **Ägyptisches Museum** across from Charlottenburg Palace (itself a museum) in the western part of the city. The Bode Museum in the eastern part of Berlin has another Egyptian collection. Other Berlin museums display everything from Islamic art to devices used to escape East Berlin and penetrate the infamous Wall (the **Haus am Checkpoint Charlie** museum).

The themes and subjects of Germany's public and private museums can be quite specialized. The German Hunting Museum (**das Deutsche Jagdmuseum**) in Munich is devoted solely to hunting-related exhibits. It contains hunting weapons, hunting sleds, antler trophies, and other objects related to hunting. Berlin's **Musikinstrumenten Museum** dates back to 1888 and, like many German museums, charges no admission to view its pianos, violins, zithers, trumpets, and more exotic instruments. The German Hygiene Museum is in Dresden. A museum devoted entirely to the fine art of building a better mousetrap is located in Neroth. Less unusual are the museums related to Germany's film tradition located in Potsdam, Munich, and Frankfurt.

52. NAMES

German names, both first and last, can be a problem for English-speakers. Especially on the phone, but also face to face, a German name can sometimes sound like Chinese to an American or Briton. (German-speakers answer the phone by saying their last name.) Knowing your ABC's in German (AH, BAY, SAY) will at least give you a way to spell out the name if need be. After a while, the more common names will become familiar. Many German names, after all, are not that different from English names: Johann (Hans) is John, and Schmidt is Smith. (But there is more than one way to spell even Schmidt—Schmitt and Schmid being just two others.)

Germans are used to being regulated in many areas of daily life that Americans might find rather repressive. Want to name your baby? Better pick a name that the local **Standesamt** (office of vital statistics) agrees with. If they don't agree to register the name you picked, you have to appeal the decision. By German law a child's name has to meet two conditions: (1) it must reflect the sex of the child, and (2) it must not endanger the "well-being of the child." A German couple who wanted to honor their favorite actress, Whoopi Goldberg, by naming their child Whoopi had their application rejected because, among other things, the name resembles the English expression "making whoopee." Another daughter from a mixed Chinese-German marriage was to receive the name Fae-Schüe. The **Standesamt** did not approve the name until it had first checked with the Chinese embassy to verify that the name was indeed a common Chinese name meaning "snowflake."

As a result of this kind of control, most Germans end up with rather conventional first names such as Julia, Julian, Phillip, Maria, Maximilian, Lisa, Christian, Franziska, and Sebastian. The name Kevin recently became more popular again with the success of movies like "Home Alone" and "Dances with Wolves" (Kevin Costner). The name earlier had also enjoyed some popularity because of the British soccer star Kevin Keegan, who played for Hamburg SV.

Hyphenated, double first names have always been very popular, especially for males. Many Germans, whether unknown or famous, answer to double names: Hans-Dietrich (Genscher), Hans Joachim (Kulenkampff), Ernst-Dieter (Lueg), Johannes Mario (Simmel), Hans-Ulrich (Klose), Max Dietrich (Kley), Uwe-Karsten (Heye) are a few names seen in the newspaper from time to time. Hans-Georg, Hans-Peter, and Karlheinz (Karl + Heinz) are among common double names for boys. Double names for girls are more rare, but the German violinist Anne-Sophie Mutter is one example. No matter what the first name might be, Austrians, Germans, and Swiss are not likely to use it.

53. NEUTRALITY

While the two Germanys were strong players on opposite sides of the Cold War, the other two major German-speaking countries, Austria and Switzerland, have a tradition of neutrality. For Switzerland, neutrality has been a success story since 1815, when the Congress of Vienna imposed the policy on the tiny Alpine nation. Austria's neutral tradition is much younger. Although the Allies insisted on it, the Republic of Austria, created in 1955 following the disastrous end of World War II, adopted neutrality also out of an abhorrence for what the war had done to a Nazi-aligned Austria, and as a practical policy for a small country of less than 7 million inhabitants. Unlike Switzerland, however, Austria became an early member of the United Nations, despite declaring its "permanent neutrality." Austria's army (**Bundesheer**) is considered a force to help ensure the country's neutrality, but Austria is excluded from joining any military alliances, and no foreign military bases are allowed on Austrian territory. The recent step of joining the European Union in 1995 will probably force Austria to modify its neutrality policy, one of the reasons that Swiss voters have declined EU membership so far.

54. NUMBERS, WEIGHTS, AND MEASURES

Americans have, for the most part, successfully defended themselves against the system of measurement used in most of the world. With only an occasional metric slip (the liter bottle, marijuana by the kilo, milligrams of medicine), Americans go about their business using those arcane, obsolete units of measurement known as *Fahrenheit, inches, feet, miles, ounces* and *pounds*. It is only when they venture out of the country that Americans have to deal with the reality that they are virtually alone when it comes to shunning the metric system used by the rest of the world.

When a German goes to the **Post** the letter's postage will be determined in grams (one gram = .035 ounces). When an Austrian pumps some gas (**Benzin**) he pays by the liter (one U.S. gallon = 3.785 liters). When a Swiss checks the air in her tires, the pressure is measured in **bar**, rather than pounds per square inch (psi). Instead of acres, a field's area will be measured in **Hektar** (one hectare = 2.4711 acres). Note also that Europeans use commas in numbers where we use periods, and vice versa. The American **23,500** is **23.500** (or **23 500**) in Europe; the decimal figure for **pi** is written as **3,14** in German, and spoken as "**drei Komma eins vier**."

Europeans use the thumb to indicate the number "one" and the thumb and index finger to indicate "two." You will confuse people in the German-speaking world if you use American hand signs for numbers. Similarly Europeans always cross the numeral "seven" to avoid confusion with "one," which resembles an American seven.

A European billion is one million millions, while in America a billion is one thousand millions. Even though German has the word **Billion**, the accurate German word for an American billion is **eine Milliarde**. An American trillion is a German **Billion**. German-speakers use the plural form **Millionen** (millions) for specific amounts when there's more than one million. So, it's **eine Million Mark** (one million marks) but **drei Millionen Mark** (3 million marks, or 3 millions).

A **Kilogramm** is 2.2046 U.S. pounds (2.2 lbs will usually be close enough). The German **Pfund** (pound) is 500 grams (500 **Gramm**, one-half of a kilogram) or 1.1 U.S. pounds. The informal term **Pfund** is often used for grocery shopping in Germany. Legally, prices must be displayed in grams or kilograms, as in "**Bohnen 1 kg DM12,90**" ("beans, 1 kilo for 12.90 marks") or "**Schweizer Emmentaler 100g DM2,99**" (Swiss cheese, 100g for 2.99 marks).

Distances are measured in kilometers. A kilometer is 0.621 mile. To convert kilometers to miles in your head, just multiply by six and drop the last number. If the sign says "50 km" that would be 6 x 50 or 300. Drop the last digit and you have 30 miles. (The exact answer is 31 miles.)

55. PATRIOTISM AND NATIONALISM

For Americans it is surprising to discover that most Germans are uncomfortable with flag-waving patriotism and nationalism. Generally, the younger the German, the more uncomfortable. Patriotism for most Austrians, Germans, and Swiss is local more than national. A Swiss holds more allegiance to his canton (state) and region than to Switzerland. An Austrian identifies strongly with his **Bundesland** (province). This has been called **Lokalpatriotismus** or **Provinzpatriotismus**. But it is the Germans, more than any others in the

German-speaking world, who are most reluctant to display any nationalistic tendencies. This does not mean that Germans don't like
their country. A 1994 survey found that 85 percent of Germans would
prefer to stay in their country rather than live in any other. Of the
15 percent who preferred another country, most—17 percent—chose
the U.S. Spain came in second with 13 percent.

Although there have been German patriots in the past, such as
the poetic Prussian Ernst Arendt, who urged his compatriots to rid
themselves of the French during the Napoleonic era, and German
imperialistic/nationalistic outbursts, as in the Bismarck or Nazi eras,
Germans today are generally uncomfortable with overt, external signs
of patriotism. In part, this is due to the past excesses of the Third Reich
and lingering feelings of Holocaust guilt. The recent post-unification
displays of skinhead, neo-Nazi nationalistic fanaticism make the great
majority of Germans very uneasy. Nor will you find the German
flag in the nation's school rooms, or even in front of the schools. It
is difficult to find the national banner flying in Germany at all, unless
you visit some government buildings, and sometimes not even then.
You certainly won't see the German flag waving atop practically
every tall building, as in the U.S.

German discomfort about increasing nationalistic tendencies can
be seen in the recent words of its politicians. Roman Herzog, upon
taking his oath of office as Germany's new president on July 1, 1994,
felt obliged to urge his countrymen to show nervous neighbors they
have nothing to fear from a bigger, stronger, united Germany, to
make foreigners feel truly welcome, and not to get carried away by
nationalistic pride. His respected predecessor, Richard von Weiz-
säcker, during his ten years in the largely ceremonial office, continu-
ally reminded Germans of the need to confront the Nazi past.

This German obsession with the past, particularly the Hitler-past,
seems extreme. But the modern German aversion to any direct involvement in world events or to showing any sign of a "national" presence
at home or abroad—in fact their tendency to be almost fanatically unpa-
triotic—all reflects German history. The German reluctance to "show
the flag" comes out of this historical uniqueness, and has continued
despite German reunification and recent outbreaks of rightist (national-

istic) extremism. The Germans, once feared for their aggressive tendencies, have become the ultimate pacifists. Their only aggression today can be seen during vacation time, when hordes of teutonic tourists invade Mediterranean beaches, and parts of Spain—the Balearics and the Canaries—come to resemble a German colony. But there is increasing pressure from outside Germany to encourage the Germans to do just what the Allies wanted to stop them from doing after World War II, to take an active political and military role in European and world affairs. Germany, reluctantly or not, is being forced to become a key player in Europe and NATO. As Europe's largest and richest nation, Germany will find it difficult not to do so in the future.

56. POLICE

Austria's rural police are called the **Gendarmerie**, a French term going back to Austrian imperial times. In German-speaking Switzerland there are two main kinds of police, the cantonal (state) police and the local police. The police (**Polizei**) in Germany are divided into several types. **Die Kripo (Kriminalpolizei)** deals only with more serious criminal cases. Traffic offenses and minor disturbances of the peace are handled by the **Schupo (Schutzpolizei)**, more like the officer on the beat in the U.S. In general, police officers are the concern of the 16 states (**Länder**). Each of Germany's states is responsible for maintaining a police force. Even the city police fall under the control of each **Land**. On the highways and autobahns the **Autobahnpolizei**—similar to the state highway patrol in the U.S., if not quite as visible—has responsibility for accidents and catching speeders and other traffic violators.

The federal police agency, the **Bundeskriminalamt** (BKA), is modeled after the American FBI and has its headquarters in Wiesbaden. The BKA handles counterfeiting, bank robbery, kidnapping, and other serious federal crimes. The **Bundesgrenzschutz** (BGS) is the German border patrol, responsible for keeping Germany's borders under control, a job that has become increasingly difficult on the eastern boundaries, following reunification and the opening up of borders in the European Union. The national railway, the Deutsche Bahn AG (formerly the Bundesbahn) also has its own police, the **Bahnpolizei**.

Complicating matters somewhat, is the action taken by some of the states in eliminating the distinction between the **Schupo** and the **Kripo**. The states of Lower Saxony, Schleswig-Holstein, and Baden-Württemberg have followed the lead of North Rhine-Westphalia in taking this controversial step. The head of the national organization for **Kripo** officers has criticized the move as a weakening of efforts against organized crime, which he claims cannot be fought by "the policeman on the street." But the states believe that there are "too many chiefs and not enough Indians" and want to put more of the current adminis-trators out on the street, leaving the **Kripo** to deal with major crime.

German police have been embarrassed by several incidents in recent years, the most notorious being the "Dagobert" case. Dagob-ert is the German name for Disney's Scrooge McDuck character. Beginning in 1988 an extortionist calling himself "Dagobert" in his extortion notes had threatened large German department stores in several cities with bombs if they didn't pay him $300,000. A bomb did $4.5 million worth of damage to the sports section of **KaDeWe** (**Kaufhaus des Westens**), Germany's largest department store, lo-cated in Berlin. The money was paid, but it was to be the last. After six more years of frustrating the police and five unsuccessful extortion attempts against other department stores, "Uncle Scrooge" finally made the mistake the police had been hoping for. Dagobert, who actually turned out to be 44-year-old Arno Funke, made another attempt to get the first extortion money since his one Berlin success. He was apprehended as he left a telephone booth in the Treptow section of Berlin. Funke had just completed a phone call demanding 1.4 million marks from the Karstadt department store headquarters in Hamburg. It must have caused the police even more frustration when in March 1995 a Berlin court sentenced Funke to less than eight years in prison, taking into consideration his supposedly diminished capacity brought on by inhaling fumes in his job as a varnisher.

57. THE POST OFFICE (*die Post*)

Dealing with the typical large post office in Germany can be confusing. Except in the tiniest, remote, small town **Post**, you will face a bewildering choice of numerous windows with strange words and phrases above them: **Postwertzeichen** (stamps), **Postsparkasse** (postal savings bank), **Einschreiben** (registered mail), **Pakete** (packages), and more. Each of these means that certain types of postal business can be transacted only at certain windows, and even if you once had a year or two of German, none of the words over the window were ever in the book.

In the fall of 1994, yellow and black ads for the Bundespost appeared in German periodicals announcing that there soon would be a "girl for everything" (**Mädchen für alles**, girl Friday) at every window of the post office. The ad went on to say that the word "girl" shouldn't be taken too seriously, but that they were very serious about the "everything." It was the Postdienst's way of introducing the "universal window," at which customers could take care of any postal business, without worrying about which window to go to. New, computerized technology called EPOS was going to help make Europe's largest postal system the best. So, if all goes according to plan, future visits to a German post office could be a lot more like a visit to a U.S. post office, in that you won't have to decide which window you need.

In January 1995, the German Bundespost's postal division became a government-owned corporation known as **Deutsche Post AG**. The German government is in the process of privatizing the postal service and splitting up the three former Bundespost divisions: postal, telecommunications, and banking.

As in the rest of Europe, the post office in Austria, Germany, and Switzerland is also the place to go to send a telegram, a fax, pay your radio and television fees, transact postal savings business, and more. (See **Point 70, Telecommunications** for more about this aspect of the postal service.)

❁

58. THE PRESS

The best-read citizens among the German-speaking countries are in Switzerland, with a newspaper circulation rate of 471 per 1000. Germany follows with 417, and Austria's rate is 389 per 1000. (The U.S. rate is 255 per 1000; Sweden boasts the world's highest rate of 580 newspapers per 1000 population.) Since 1975 the Austrian government has supported the press financially, subsidizing Austrian newspaper publishers to the tune of 214 million schillings (about $25.6 million) in 1992 alone. Except for lower postal rates for periodicals, neither Germany nor Switzerland do the same, leaving their periodicals to compete in the journalistic marketplace.

Probably the best-known German-language news magazine is *Der Spiegel*. This Hamburg weekly, modeled after *Time* magazine, began publishing in 1945 and has become one of Europe's most important periodicals, with a circulation of around one million. A young upstart competitor, *Focus*, began publishing its more flashy version of the news in Munich in 1993, soon reaching a circulation figure almost half that of the more liberal *Der Spiegel*. Austria's own news magazine is *profil*, with a circulation of about 100,000, and a reputation for hard-hitting journalism.

The largest German-language daily newspapers are Germany's tabloid *Bildzeitung* (Hamburg) with a national circulation of 4.5 million, the influential *Frankfurter Allgemeine Zeitung* (390,000 circ.), Austria's *Neue Kronen Zeitung* (Vienna, 1 million circ.), and Zurich's *Neue Zürcher Zeitung*.

Freedom of the press is a guarantee found in the constitution of each of the German-speaking countries, but the way in which this guarantee is actually carried out differs from country to country. Austria has one of the more interesting approaches, guaranteeing the right of individuals to have a rejoinder or rebuttal (**Entgegnung**) published in a magazine, newspaper, or broadcast on radio or television. If a statement appears that ostensibly defames a person or public body, or gives inaccurate information concerning them, they have the right to a rebuttal. Under the 1982 Media Law (**Mediengesetz**), which updated an older Press Law, the rejoinder must be true and may deal only with factual reporting, not opinions. Austria's Media

Law thus tries to protect the rights of the individual while at the same time supporting journalistic rights and freedom of the press. Many of the provisions of Austria's Media Law would seem overly restrictive to journalists in the U.S. and Great Britain. A public person's intimate "sphere of purely private life" is off limits, for example. A fine of up to 50,000 Austrian schillings ($5,000) can be imposed for publishing information on a person's family life, health, or sexual relations. But Austrians point to tabloid abuses concerning the British royal family and the O.J. Simpson trial circus as examples of why their law makes sense. (No television, film, or live coverage of court proceedings is allowed in Austria, Germany or Switzerland.)

Article 5 of the German **Grundgesetz** (constitution) guarantees freedom of the press and the right of access to information. Germany ranks among the few countries of the world that observe true, uncensored freedom of the press. At the same time, however, German newspapers, much more so than their U.S. counterparts, are generally expected to have a particular political viewpoint. Various newspapers and magazines are openly labeled liberal, conservative, far right, far left, or somewhere in between. German readers, perhaps far more than American readers, seem to be much more aware of the political leanings of their periodicals. Journalists in Germany do not try to be the "unbiased" and "objective" observers that U.S. journalists claim to be.

59. THE PRISON SYSTEM

Germans may wonder about some of their judges and courts, but Germany's prisons hold only a fraction of the number of criminals incarcerated in the United States, and inmates serve much shorter terms. Prison overcrowding is rarely a problem in Germany. There were approximately 48,000 prisoners in western Germany's 170 jails in 1993—a mere 75 percent occupancy rate. The state of Florida alone, with a population of just 13 million (in comparison to western Germany's 60 million) had an incarcerated population of some 50,000 at the same time. The German figure would have been even lower without several thousand rejected asylum-seekers awaiting deportation. Consider these recent comparative incarceration rates (per 100,000 population): United States, 519; Canada, 116; Germany, 80.

The low incarceration rate in Germany, of course, reflects a more homogeneous population than that of the U.S. Germans tend to be law-abiding. It also reflects a basic philosophy that is part of German law: a prison sentence is the punishment of last resort. German law does require that people convicted of a felony (**Verbrechen**) must be given a prison sentence, but probation is possible for sentences of under two years. The great majority of offenders convicted of a misdemeanor (**Vergehen**) end up paying only a fine. (See also **Points 16, The Court System; 17** and **18** for more on **Crime and Punishment**.)

60. PRIVACY

Doors and windows in the German-speaking world are built like bank vaults compared to their flimsy U.S. counterparts. A solid, well-crafted German door is a sign of the importance that German-speaking people attach to their privacy. The roll-down metal shutters that cover German windows at night are another. Solid fences, walls, or thick hedges separate and define one neighbor's yard from the other's. German neighbors usually don't make an effort to become better acquainted, even after years of living next door. Doors inside houses and offices are usually closed, silently saying, "Please knock before entering." Door locks are usually double locks requiring keys that are a locksmith's dream and a burglar's nightmare.

A German's house is truly his castle, and it is a very private castle. Whether you are a friend, relative, business associate, or exchange student, being invited to visit or stay in a German family's home is a special honor. Germans are almost fanatic about their privacy and do not casually invite people over, even just for dinner. Guests show their appreciation of a valued invitation by bringing a gift of flowers, wine, or candy for the hosts.

Americans find it difficult and slow-going to make friends with

Germans, Austrians, or Swiss. While Germans can be quite cordial, the pace of opening up and making contacts is much slower than in the U.S. Even Germans who move to a new town in Germany may have problems in this regard, because a German's social network tends to be small and not readily open to expansion. Though they like to travel for vacations, and despite a slight increase in mobility in recent years, people in the German world generally are not very mobile, preferring the security of staying in their home town (**Heimatstadt**). In initial contacts, German-speakers tend to be cordial while maintaining their distance. Americans may often misinterpret this reticence as unfriendly behavior. It may take longer, but once a friendship has been established, it will usually be deeper and less superficial than a typical American relationship. This cultural trait extends to the German language and the use of the formal you (**Sie**) with anyone outside of the sphere of family and close friends, even for people a German-speaker has known for years.

61. PUBLIC TRANSPORTATION

Most cities of any size in German Europe have an excellent public transportation system, often consisting of a mixture of buses, street cars, and subways. The German cities of Berlin, Frankfurt am Main, Hamburg, Stuttgart, and Munich, as well as Vienna in Austria also have excellent underground and commuter trains. The underground train or subway is called the **U-Bahn** and is designated by a circular sign with a large blue "U." Commuter lines are called the **S-Bahn**, and are indicated by a big green "S." Many other cities have extensive streetcar routes in addition to buses.

Tickets for buses, streetcars, or trains usually need to be purchased prior to boarding. This is done at a ticket office or from a vending machine. Most cities have a special multiple ticket that saves money by offering four or five tickets in a strip (**Streifenkarte** or **Sammelkarte**). A ticket is not valid until it has been canceled by insertion into a yellow or red stamp machine called an **Entwerter** or **Entgelter**. The **Entwerter**, located either on the platform at a station or in the train or bus itself, stamps a code on the ticket. Tickets are not regularly checked in the honor system that is used in most cities, but random spot checks are made, and anyone without a valid (canceled) ticket or pass must pay a fine on the spot.

62. RADIO AND TELEVISION

It was not until 1987 that German television viewers had the option of viewing anything other than the three public TV channels (ARD, ZDF and the "Third Program" regional channels). Radio was similarly limited to three stations, even in large German cities. Austria and Switzerland were even more limited. Even today the Austrian TV network ORF offers viewers a choice of only two television channels. Switzerland's single DRS German television channel only began its all-day broadcasts in 1993. (Switzerland also has channels for French and Italian.) Viewers with cable or satellite TV can watch a variety of private channels; in Germany, some private channels, such as RTL, also broadcast over the air. Cable and satellite viewers can watch CNN, MTV Europe, n-tv (the German CNN), Premiere (movies, David Letterman, and "Saturday Night Live"), VIVA (the German response to MTV), NBC Super Channel ("Tonight Show"), movie and sports channels, and more. 3Sat is the satellite version of programming from the Austrian, Swiss, and German networks combined. About half of the satellite channels are scrambled, requiring monthly fees.

To help finance the public radio and television stations, the Austrian, German, and Swiss governments collect fees (in reality a type of tax) for the use of radio and television sets. In Germany each household pays a single fee, no matter how many radios or TV sets there may be in the house, but children with their own income pay an additional fee. It doesn't matter who owns the device, the determining factor is who has access to the radio or TV. If you have a car radio, there is no extra fee, provided you or your spouse are already paying the household fee and the car is registered in your name. Portable radios used mostly at home are exempt. Most people pay their **Rundfunkgebühren** by automatic withdrawal (**Lastschrift**) from their bank account. Fees can be paid annually, every six months, or quarterly. The forms for registering a radio or TV can be picked up at any post office.

In 1997 the German radio/TV monthly fee amounted to 28.25 DM (about $16.00) for a household with both radio and television receivers. Although ARD used to receive 70 percent and ZDF 30 percent of these license fees, now this income is split evenly between the two public networks. Additional revenue comes from both radio and television advertising. (Switzerland allows no advertising on public radio.) Broadcast advertising on the public television channels is very restricted, with no advertising allowed on Sunday, and no TV ads after 8:00 p.m. or during a program. TV ads appear in 5 or 10-minute blocks. On the German commercial channels, the constant barrage of advertising is as bad or worse than in the U.S.

Europe had TV stereo sound long before the U.S. If you have a stereo TV set, you can listen to beautiful stereo sound, and some shows can be heard with either the dubbed German or the original English soundtrack. ARD also shows movies with dual sound, offering a choice of German or the original language. In some parts of Germany and in some hotels, you can also watch French television (via cable or with a converter).

There are also German versions of American shows such as "Family Feud" (*Familienduell*) and "The Price is Right" (*Der Preis ist heiß*). Bert and Ernie teach German preschoolers the ABC's in German on the long-running *Sesamstraße*. The "Columbo" series with Peter Falk is so well-known in Germany that director Wim Wenders included Falk and some "Columbo" humor in two of his recent movies.

Of course, the Germans have many television shows of their own. These include variety shows (a TV genre hardly ever seen in the U.S. today), the popular, long-running series *Lindenstraße*, comedies (*Deutschland lacht*), dramas, detective shows (*Derrick, Der Alte, Tatort*), documentaries, soap operas (*Gute Zeiten, schlechte Zeiten*, "Good Times,

Bad Times''), interview shows (*Der heiße Stuhl*, "The Hot Seat''), and others.

The German PAL color TV standard, used throughout most of Europe, is incompatible with TV sets and video cassettes from non-PAL countries such as France and the United States.

63. REGIONS

Even as the Germans have become somewhat more mobile, moving around more than in the past, they still usually identify first with their region—**Schwaben** (Swabia), **Oberbayern** (Upper Bavaria), etc. This regional identity goes back more than a thousand years to a time when the Germanic tribes—Alamanni (Swabians), Franks, Frisians, Bavarians, Saxons, Thuringians—were scattered across the area of Europe now known as Austria, Switzerland, France (**Frankreich**), and Germany.

German regionalism does not always correspond to the **Länder** boundaries. Germany's 16 states, even the "older" 11 original states of former West Germany, are newer creations invented after World War II, only partly following traditional regional borders. Americans are puzzled by the fact that Germans don't even use the state names in their mailing addresses, until they realize that the German states (**Bundesländer**), most of which were first created in 1949, are largely a matter of administrative convenience. Bavaria and the Hanseatic city-states of Bremen and Hamburg are among the few exceptions, having long histories of an independent existence. Often it is difficult to see the road signs that designate the border between one **Bundesland** and another. Such signs did not exist until fairly recently.

In Austria and Switzerland the story of local pride is much the same, although the various provinces have been around much longer. The Swiss take great pride in their regional differences and give a great deal of autonomy to each of the 26 cantons. In Austria the nine **Bundesländer** are each very much aware of their own identities and characteristics. There is a lot of rivalry between the capital city of

Vienna and the rest of Austria, a situation arising out of Austria's imperial past and the former importance of Vienna.

64. RELIGION

Germany and Switzerland are each about half Protestant (**evangelisch**) and half Roman Catholic (**katholisch**). Austria is about 86 percent Roman Catholic. In all three countries there are small minorities representing other faiths, including Jews, Muslims, Mormons, and others. Particularly in Germany, there are also those who claim no religion, sometimes to avoid the mandatory church tax (**Kirchensteuer**) collected by the government to support the various churches.

Despite the high percentage of nominal Catholics and Protestants, very few Germans, Austrians, and Swiss regularly attend church. For the most part, the social aspects of church attendance, common in America, are not present in Europe. Although there are some exceptions, church in Europe, including German-speaking Europe, is more formal and ceremonial. Regular church-goers tend to be older people. For most people, church attendance is a special event reserved for religious holidays, baptisms, marriages, and funerals.

This does not mean that religion is not an important part of life for German speakers. In fact, beginning with religious reformers like the German **Martin Luther** (1483-1546) and the Swiss German **Huldrich Zwingli** (1484-1531), many of the world's best known religious philosophers and intellectuals have come from the German part of Europe. In more recent times these have included influential theologians such as the Swiss Calvinist **Karl Barth** (1886-1968), the German Lutheran **Rudolf Karl Bultmann** (1884-1976), the Austrian-Israeli **Martin Buber** (1878-1965), the Swiss rebel Catholic **Hans Küng** (1928-   ), whose challenge to the infallibility of the Pope led to a controversial ban on his right to teach Catholic theology, and the German-American **Paul Tillich** (1886-1965), whose philosophy calling for a blending of religion and secular society compelled him to leave Nazi Germany. Many courageous priests, pastors, and

theologians—like the German **Dietrich Bonhoeffer** (1906-1945)—
died at the hands of the Nazis because they stood by their conviction
that the church should not divorce itself from politics. In the years
leading up to the collapse of the Berlin Wall, the Lutheran churches
in former East Germany became "underground" centers for those
activists who wanted to reform that country's government.

65. REUNIFICATION

From the beginning, Germany has been a fragmented land, and it
has continued to have problems staying in one piece, primarily as
the result of wars (most self-inflicted). When it ended in 1945, World
War II and its political aftermath left Germany shattered once again.
The Germans refer to this point in their history as "**Stunde Null**,"
the "zero hour." Many books have been written on the significance
of the cataclysmic "**Stunde Null**" in modern German history.

Almost exactly 40 years after its creation in 1949, the Federal
Republic of Germany was to have yet another "zero hour," this
time known as the "**Wende**," the German word for "turning point."
Germans now use this word to refer to the historical turning point
in 1989 when the Berlin Wall fell, opening the way for the two Germa-
nies to again become one. This second "zero hour" was in some
ways just as traumatic as the first.

Little did the East Germans at the November 4th mass demonstration on East Berlin's **Alexanderplatz** realize how soon their revolution would be preempted by the uncontrollable chain of events they
had set in motion. The 17 million East Germans were soon steamrol-
lered by 62 million West Germans and their leader, Helmut Kohl.
Pleas to look at alternatives to total unification were drowned out in
the frenzied rush toward a "United Fatherland." Günter Grass,
the prize-winning West German novelist, was labeled a traitor for
pushing the idea of a looser German confederation that would allow
the East Germans to guide their own revolution and create their own
brand of German democracy. But it was not to be. The holes in the
Wall were like holes in a bursting dam.

It was the inability of the East German government to trust its own citizens, and forty years of inconsistencies that finally led to the fall of the German Democratic Republic. The East's isolation was invaded by western television and western ideas that only highlighted the many illogical contradictions and the rot in the East German system. Housing rents may have been extremely low, but it took a ten-year wait and 15,000 east marks, or over a year's salary to buy a Trabant, a car that was inferior in every way to those in the West. It was a "classless" society in which the party leaders and top government officials were more equal than others.

In spite of Germany's celebrated reunification on October 3, 1990, there are, in many ways, still two Germanys. The dizzying speed with which reunification took place had led some to expect overnight changes in a system that took 40 years to create. It is taking more time and suffering than many realized. The former East Germans are now paying the price for the failure of a planned economy that was neither well-planned nor well-managed. The western Germans, who after the first decade of the Wall never really thought that reunification was truly possible, underestimated the time and costs required to rebuild a dilapidated East Germany and bring together two countries that had gone their separate ways for 40 years. Germans on both sides of the former Wall, who tend to be overly pessimistic, now talk of "the Wall in the head" ("**die Mauer im Kopf**") that continues to divide them.

There are difficulties. Unemployment in the East remains high, businesses have disappeared, there are differences in income, along with philosophical and political differences, and taxes have gone up to pay for unification. But no one really wants to go back, even if they could. Some estimates say it will take a generation before things become "normal" in the two halves of Germany. Others point to the German "economic miracle" ("**Wirtschaftswunder**") of the post-war era, claiming it proves that normalcy will happen sooner. But it will take time to bring together people who developed different societies over four decades.

66. SCIENCE AND TECHNOLOGY

Over the ages, the German-speaking world has been a vital contributor to the development of science and technology. The German Johannes Gutenberg invented movable type and modern printing around 1450. In the 16th century the German Swiss Paracelsus was already working on the chemical and medical theories that would later form the basis for modern biology, chemistry, and medicine. Johannes Kepler, a German astronomer and mathematician, accurately measured planetary motion in the 17th century. The Austrian monk Gregor Mendel developed the first laws of genetics in 1856. Albert Einstein, born in Ulm, Germany in 1879, first published his theory of relativity in 1905. In counting Nobel Prizes just in the fields of chemistry, physics, and medicine since 1905, the Austrians have garnered 13, the Germans more than 30, and the Swiss no less than 14.

All three German-speaking countries have a reputation for their scientific and technological prowess, especially in turbogenerators, textile machines, tunnel building, optics, chemicals, cable lifts, automobiles, and high-speed trains. The Swedish-Swiss multinational firm of Asea Brown Bovery (ABB) is known for its turbogenerators and other advanced technology. The German Daimler-Benz Aerospace AG (Dasa) constructs aircraft, satellites, and is involved in other areas of aerospace. Daimler and ABB recently merged their train production. Hoechst AG, Germany's largest chemical company, is one of the largest in the world; Hoechst has bought Dow Chemical in the U.S. Austria's state-owned VOEST-Alpine group sells its technology in construction, engineering, steel, trains, and hydroelectric power production all over the world.

Ironically, for a country so identified with invention and technological prowess, a recent survey shows that Germans tend to be uncomfortable with technology in its everyday forms. Only 22 percent feel at home with a computer, 33 percent with a video recorder, and just 19 percent with an answering machine. Americans, Britons, and the French all rank higher in their technology comfort levels, with Americans at the top. (At home with computers: 54 percent; VCRs: 77 percent; answering machines: 63 percent.) However, this may not be quite so ironic if we remember that German is the language that gave us the word "klutz" (via Yiddish; German **Klotz**, a block of wood, a clumsy blockhead). But paradoxically Germans are the most positive when asked if technology makes life better.

67. SHOPPING

Shoppers in the German-speaking countries have to put up with very limited store hours—among the most restrictive in Europe.

Matters improved somewhat in 1996 when Germany's legislators finally granted the country's shoppers a long-awaited wish. Beginning November 1, 1996, store owners who wanted to could remain open between the hours of 6:00 a.m. and 8:00 p.m. on weekdays and until 4:00 p.m. on Saturdays (previously only allowed on the first Saturday of each month, the so-called **langer Samstag**). Sundays remain a legal day of rest for almost all merchants, but for the first time bakeries are now allowed to make and sell fresh bread and rolls on Sunday and open an hour earlier (at 5:30 a.m.) every day. Having the new law go into effect just before Christmas helped ease the transition because stores have long been allowed to stay open longer during the four weeks prior to the big gift-giving holiday.

It may still be too early to celebrate Germany's new shopping freedom. How much more shopping time Germans actually get still depends on union agreements and propietors' inclinations. A few years ago when stores were granted the right to stay open until 8:00 p.m. on Thursdays, most smaller shops continued to close their doors by 6:00 p.m. Even some bigger enterprises and department stores failed to take advantage of the longer hours allowed on Thursdays and Saturdays. Of the 68.5 shopping hours per week then allowed by law, the average German shopkeeper kept his doors open only 52 hours a week.

"Never on Sunday" could be the motto of merchants in Germany. Sunday is truly a day of rest. In Germany virtually nothing is open for business, but in Austria there is a trend for more stores opening on Sunday. In Germany there are a few exceptions for tourism, but on the whole, don't plan on buying anything on Sunday.

Gas stations, restaurants, and other food and drink establishments are about the only place you can spend your money until Monday morning. There have actually been lawsuits in Germany over this small remaining loophole, complaining that train station shops and some service station minimarts were actually selling to people who were not train passengers or weren't buying gas for their cars, as stipulated in Germany's strict **Ladenschluß** (store closing) laws. In 1993 Germany's highest administrative court established the legality of such after-hour sales of "travel necessities" by minimarts, some of which make about a third of their sales to walk-up customers.

The German-speaking world seems to have adopted a consumer philosophy that is the exact opposite of the U.S. slogan, "The customer is always right." In the name of protecting the German worker, Germany's unions and shopkeepers have conspired since 1956 to create store hours that favor the store owners and employees over the customer.

Smaller shops and banks in the German-speaking countries are often closed between noon and 2:00 p.m., but larger stores and most department stores stay open at that time, indicated by signs reading "**durchgehend geöffnet**." Stores and banks almost always have their opening hours displayed on the door, so you can check on this in advance.

Marktplatz (market square) open-air markets are fun to visit. Selling everything from food to flowers, pottery to pans, and more, these wonderful institutions can be found on Saturday in every Austrian, German, or Swiss community of any size. In some towns and cities the markets are a daily occurrence located on a central square, often around a cathedral or church. And on Sunday, in almost any larger German city, you will find popular flea markets set up along some street, boulevard, or in a park. Stretching sometimes for many blocks, the **Flohmarkt** offers new and used products, antiques, furniture, and knickknacks of all sorts.

Department stores in Austria, Germany, and Switzerland are much like their American counterparts. The main difference reflects the general European practice of having large grocery sections and popular cafeterias in department stores. Often some of the best restaurants in a city are the dining facilities in department stores. Gourmet shoppers often head for their local **Kaufhaus** to find food and drink of all kinds. Germany's largest and best-known department store is the giant KaDeWe (KAH-DAY-VAY, Kaufhaus des Westens) in Berlin. On the sixth floor of KaDeWe there is an amazing array of gourmet foods. The largest store of its kind in continental Europe (only Harrod's of London is larger), KaDeWe is owned by the Hertie chain of department stores. Other well-known German chains include Karstadt, Kaufhof, and Horten.

American Express, Visa, and MasterCard are widely accepted in Germany, Austria and Switzerland, but some stores insist on a minimum amount (usually 100 DM, about $65) for credit card transactions. Credit card use in Europe is much lower than in the U.S. While it is rare to find a store or restaurant in the U.S. that does not accept credit cards, in Germany it is sometimes difficult to find one that does. There are good reasons for this: (1) A European credit card is more like a debit card; the cardholder has little choice in paying the full balance, as this is done automatically by the bank that issued the card. (2) In Germanic culture, debt is viewed as a sin; the German word for debt, **Schuld**, also means "guilt." (3) Perhaps because of reason number two, it is more difficult to obtain credit in Europe than in the U.S., and borrowing money with a credit card is to be avoided—even for a short-term loan. Whether for a house or a car, Europeans also have to pay a bigger down payment—a third or more—on a loan, reflecting the Germanic reluctance to incur debt.

When making purchases, be aware that all the German-speaking countries levy a value-added tax (VAT, **Mehrwertsteuer**) on the price of goods and services. The VAT is a type of sales tax already included in the price of anything you buy, not added on as in the U.S. The standard VAT is 20 percent in Austria, 16 percent in Germany, and 6.2 percent in Switzerland. (Under certain conditions when making larger purchases it is possible for non-Europeans to get a VAT refund, but the procedure is complex and arrangements must be made at the time of purchase.)

68. SPORTS

Americans are almost alone in the world with their lack of enthusiasm for the game known as "football" everywhere but in America, where it is called "soccer." Although the Germans know about baseball and American football, neither of these New World sports is very popular or widespread in Germany or Europe. Although an annual American football exhibition game in Berlin has become a recent tradition, German boys still grow up playing **Fußball** (soccer), not football.

In recent years, some American games have become more popular in Germany. Basketball has a reasonably large number of fans, and volleyball is also quite popular. But the king of German amateur and professional sports is definitely soccer, "**König Fußball**" ("king football"). Thousands of amateur **Fußballvereine** (soccer clubs) provide the opportunity for Germans to play soccer. As a spectator sport, soccer draws an average of over 25,000 fans to each professional game. The Germans have won the World Cup three times, the last being in 1990, when over 35 percent of the German population, almost 29 million viewers, watched the finals. In the U.S., only an estimated one million, or 0.004 percent of viewers thought the 1990 games were worth watching. The World Cup games held in the U.S. in 1994, with an estimated total world television audience of more than 32 billion (the World Series and the Super Bowl seem like mere amateur events by comparison) gave Americans a never-before-seen exposure to the game of soccer.

The German Sports Federation (**DSB, Deutscher Sportbund**) has 19 regional federations and numerous associated sports groups. The DSB, with more than two million volunteer coaches and officials, is one sign of how sports-minded the Germans are. Another is the profusion of sports facilities all over Germany—playing fields, gymnasiums, indoor and outdoor swimming pools, and even olympic training facilities. The DSB sponsors many programs aimed at physical fitness, the most famous of which is the venerable "**Trimm dich!**" campaign. "Trimm dich!" jogging paths and work-out areas are still seen all over Germany, even if the "Trimm dich!" fad of the 1970s and 1980s has faded a bit. "**Sport für Jedermann**" encourages millions of Germans to compete in track, swimming, cycling, skiing, and hiking. DSB awards gold, bronze, and silver medals to amateurs who qualify in a certain sport. About 700,000 Germans pass DSB tests to earn the **Deutsche Sportabzeichen** each year.

One out of three Germans is a member of one of the many sports clubs across Germany that offer opportunities to play soccer, handball, basketball, volleyball, tennis, and other sports. Not all are active players, but the number of Germans involved in sports is relatively high. This is all the more remarkable in light of the fact that German schools, unlike those in America, do not have interscholastic sports programs.

In Germany and the other German-speaking countries, golf is still something of an elitist sport, considered a pursuit of the well-to-do, an expensive diversion for tycoons and the upper echelons of business. Public golf courses are virtually unknown. Beautiful golf facilities can be found, but usually at a price. If you are a golf fan, your best hope is that your company can provide you access to the sport. Usually, the only alternative is to join a golf club or pay relatively high private greens fees. The German Open golf tournament is held in Düsseldorf in August.

Through the well-known successes of German tennis stars like Boris Becker, Steffi Graf, Michael Stich, and Anke Huber, tennis has become one of the most popular sports in Germany. Similar to golf, there are few public tennis courts in the German-speaking countries, but private tennis courts (indoor and out) dot the land. For an hourly fee, you can play on clay or artificial turf courts. (The asphalt courts often seen in the U.S. are very rare in Germany.) As with golf, some companies provide the perk of access to tennis. Germany's biggest tennis event is the Federation Cup, held each year in Frankfurt. The Mercedes Cup is in July in Stuttgart. The German Open is in Hamburg in May. The BMW Tennis Open is in Munich in late April. Kitzbühel, Austria hosts both the Austrian Open (July) and the Head Cup (August).

Unlike golf or tennis, it is difficult to find a German community that doesn't have a public **Schwimmbad** or swimming pool. Often there is a **Hallenbad**, an indoor pool, alongside the outdoor pool.

Larger cities may have dozens of swimming facilities in various areas. Some communities have recently had difficulty keeping up with the costs of running these aquatic arenas, raising admission fees and reducing hours of operation, but public pools are still widely available all over Germany throughout the year. Pools are sometimes also part of a public or private health spa (**Bad**).

69. SWITZERLAND (*die Schweiz*)

A close look at Swiss history leaves one amazed that Switzerland exists as a country at all. Its long history (1291 is the official date for the origins of the Swiss Confederation) is complex and fragmented, a tale of turmoil and local interests conflicting with regional and national concerns. Known today as a neutral, peaceful nation, Switzerland's past was anything but tranquil. Today's prosperous, tolerant, industrious Switzerland, partly due to the Alpine land's rugged geography, arose out of rebellion, religious strife, political discord, and recurring disunity. But a sense of common purpose and a need to stick together resulted from this frequent disharmony.

Switzerland is a country with four national languages, 26 cantons (provinces), and a population of about seven million. The Latin name of Switzerland that appears on the nation's coins and stamps is **Helvetia**, a term derived from the Celtic Helvetii who first entered the area now known as Switzerland around 100 B.C. This Latin designation avoids having to squeeze the French, German, and Italian names (**Suisse, Schweiz, Svizzera**) onto coins and stamps, and is typical of the sensible Swiss way of solving problems. Switzerland is a country that has solved the problems of multiple languages (German is spoken by 65 percent of the population; French, 18 percent; Italian, 10 percent; Romansh, one percent; other languages, 6 percent), limited natural resources and arable land, as well as geographic isolation.

The **Ewiger Bund** (Eternal League) formed by the original three cantons of Uri, Schwyz, and Unterwalden on August 1, 1291 for mutual self-defense was to become the basis for the present Swiss

Confederation or **Schweizerische Eidgenossenschaft**. Schwyz would lend its name to the entire Confederation of 26 cantons, known as **die Schweiz** in German.

Capitalizing on its traditional neutrality, Switzerland has become an important center of world organizations such as the International Red Cross (whose red cross symbol is the Swiss flag in reverse colors), headquartered in Geneva, in the French-speaking portion of the country. The famous Geneva Convention on the treatment of war-wounded and prisoners was encouraged by the Swiss in 1864. The Universal Postal Union was founded in German-speaking Bern in 1874. Switzerland joined the League of Nations in 1920 only after obtaining special recognition of its neutrality. Although not a member of the United Nations (a 1986 Swiss referendum continued this exclusion), the Swiss do participate in non-political UN organizations like UNICEF, WHO, and UNESCO. Most recently, in 1994, the Swiss, unlike their Austrian neighbors, voted against joining the European Union.

The present government of Switzerland operates under a constitution that goes back to 1874, which itself dates back to similar constitutions from 1848 and 1815.

70. TELECOMMUNICATIONS

The old **Bundespost**, Germany's postal service, was Ma Bell, AT&T, Western Union, cable TV, the corner bank, and the post office all rolled into one. In 1990, which happened to be the 500th anniversary of the German postal service, the **Bundespost** was split into three separate divisions: **Postdienst, Postbank**, and **Telekom**. The goal was to make the entire operation and each division more competitive. The **Postdienst** division of the former **Bundespost** became the new privatized **Deutsche Post AG** in 1995. In addition, the other two divisions, **Postbank** and **Telekom**, are to be privatized in the next few years, a European trend that got its start in Great Britain. The Austrian and Swiss postal systems remain entirely government run for now.

Everything that has to do with the German **Post** is painted yellow and black. The telephone division, **Deutsche Telekom**, has been introducing a more fashionable white and lavender color scheme for phone booths and service vehicles.

The **Post**, in addition to handling the mail, is also the place to go when you want to send a telegram, a fax, pay radio and television fees, make a phone call, deposit or withdraw funds to/from a postal savings account, exchange foreign money, or take out a magazine subscription. It is difficult to name something that can't be done at the **Post**.

Whether at the **Post** or in a phone booth, a German coin or card phone can be a little confusing at first glance. First, be aware that German coin-operated public phones will only accept 10-pfennig, 1-mark, and 5-mark coins. With a card phone all you have to do is insert the **Telefonkarte**, a smart card that you can buy at a discount in units of 12 or 50 marks and use until the card's value has been used up. Austria and Switzerland have similar telephone cards.

For a local call, insert three 10-pfennig coins to start. The minimum charge for a local call is 30 pfennigs (for five minutes). An indicator will show when you need to insert more coins. You have a few seconds to do so before the connection is broken. Don't insert too many coins in advance, because you can't get change for unused coins. That is one advantage of the phone card. For long distance calls, be sure to have a good supply of one-mark and five-mark coins if you're not using a **Telefonkarte**. Also note that there are phone booths marked "**Inland**" (Domestic) and "**International**." Calls to places outside of Germany can only be made from booths with the "International" designation. During normal business hours you can place calls from phone booths inside the post office and pay afterwards at a special window.

71. TERRORISM

The Irish Republican Army in Northern Ireland, the Basque separatist ETA in Spain, or the Palestinian PLO may be more notorious, but Germany and, to a lesser extent, Austria have also been subject to violent acts of terrorist rebellion and insurrection. Germany's leftist **Rote Armee Fraktion** (Red Army Faction, RAF), which dates back to the early 1970s, has had occasional dramatic success in assassinating German bankers, lawyers and industrialists. Even in very recent times, the RAF or its successors have blown up prisons and targeted the Mercedes of distinguished German symbols of power in business and government with light-activated bombs on German roads.

Germany's terrorists have tended to be well-to-do, highly educated radicals influenced by the student protest movement of the late 1960s. Rudi Dutschke (1940-1979), the leader of West Berlin's **"antiautoritär"** student movement, was gravely injured by an assassination attempt in 1968, survived, and later went on to work for the Greens. His anarchist "antiauthoritarians" created chaos on the streets of Berlin. Arising out of this radical cauldron in the early 1970s was the infamous Baader-Meinhof gang. Named for its leaders, Andreas Baader (1943-1977), the son of a university professor, and his ex-journalist girlfriend Ulrike Meinhof (1934-1976), the **Baader-Meinhof-Gruppe** called itself the Rote Armee Fraktion. Baader, Meinhof, and other RAF members were arrested in 1972, but that was not the end of the RAF. In April 1975, the RAF was responsible for a fatal attack on the German embassy in Stockholm. The German ambassador was seriously injured, two staff members were shot to death, and hostages suffered serious burns in an explosion set off by the terrorists. One RAF member was killed in the bombing and three others were jailed. Thanks to the Red Army Faction, 1977 was a particularly troublesome time for Germany. In that year alone, following Ulrike Meinhof's suicide in prison in 1976, the RAF murdered the federal prosecutor, a prominent banker, and the head of Daimler-Benz's employees organization, all symbols of German capitalism and power. Following the RAF's failed hijacking of a Lufthansa jet to Somalia, Baader and two other RAF members committed suicide in prison (or were "helped" to do so by some accounts). The Baader-Meinhof gang was gone, but the RAF has endured.

Although the RAF's terrorist attacks have been less frequent in the 1980s and 1990s, the so-called "third generation" of the Red

Army Faction has managed to continue creating headlines and to elude capture to a large extent. From 1985 to 1988 the RAF assassinated several business and government leaders, botching only a 1988 attempt to eliminate then German Secretary of the Treasury, Hans Tietmeyer. In 1989 a particularly nasty bomb trap on an open road destroyed the armored limousine of Deutsche Bank CEO Alfred Herrhausen, killing him and reminding Germans once again that the RAF was still around. Two years later Treuhand boss Detlev Karsten Rohwedder was shot to death. In March 1993 the RAF took credit for blowing up an empty, newly constructed prison south of Frankfurt, causing $70 million damage. Just a few months later, Wolfgang Grams, an RAF suspect, was killed in a police shoot-out that left Grams and a policeman dead at the once obscure train station of Bad Kleinen in eastern Germany. There was a huge outcry about the possible "execution" of Grams by the GSG-9 federal anti-terrorist police. (Germany has no death penalty.) *Der Spiegel* came out with a garish cover story that graphically showed a huge bullet wound in Grams' head. The chief of the BKA (Germany's FBI) announced that Grams had probably either committed suicide or accidentally shot himself after being shot by the police, but accusations of a cover-up by the police were soon swirling about in the German press. There was even serious talk, some called it hysteria, of disbanding the special GSG-9 police unit that had caught up with Grams in the first place. This was the same GSG-9 tactical force that had become a German legend by freeing RAF hostages in the Lufthansa hijacking in Somalia back in 1977. The incident soon cost the Minister of the Interior (**Innenminister**), Rudolf Seiters, his job. Seiters must have taken small comfort when a later independent investigation by Swiss authorities indicated there was a high probability that Grams had shot himself. During all the controversy, people seemed to forget that Grams' girlfriend, who was with him at the time of the police raid, was suspected in the 1988 attempt on Hans Tietmeyer's life. Some Germans have also been displeased to see a few former RAF terrorists— once sentenced to life terms back in the seventies—being released or being considered for parole by German courts in the 1990s, after serving terms of about 20 years.

While terrorism in Germany is largely a leftist phenomenon, with right-wing attacks against foreigners tending to come mostly from isolated individuals, Austrian terrorism comes primarily from the right. A favorite terrorist device in Austria, the letter bomb, dates back to 1935, when they were first used by a clandestine Nazi group in Salzburg to attack specific church and state officials. More recently, a group calling itself the **Bajuwarische Befreiungsarmee** (Bavarian Liberation Army, BBA), with units like the **Kampfeinheit** (combat unit) **Graf Ernst Rüdiger von Starhemberg**, has revived the letter bomb technique in Austria. (Count von Starhemberg was known for freeing Austria from the Turks.) By sending out a series of the deadly missives to targets like a TV announcer, the Austrian General Director for Public Safety, and the attorney for a previous letter-bombing suspect, this small organization, whose members seem to hate foreigners, ethnic minorities, and those who support them, has made Austrians nervous about checking their mail. But the BBA has also used pipe bombs to get its message across, one directed at a bilingual elementary school in Klagenfurt, another killing four gypsies, and a third unexploded bomb placed near a kindergarten for Croatian children. Austrian frustration over this terrorist wave has led to charges of police bungling and criticism of their failure to apprehend any BBA members.

72. TIME AND PUNCTUALITY

It is easier to understand the Germanic concept of time once you have admired an Austrian railway timetable or a German school's class schedule. Such schedules are masterpieces of planning and are definitely not just for looks. Swiss trains have been known to run late, but usually you can set your watch by their punctual arrival and departure. Travelers learn very quickly that if a Deutsche Bahn (German Rail) train schedule says the train will be in the Baden-Baden train station for exactly two minutes, they had better have their luggage gathered and be ready to get off the train before it leaves the station precisely two minutes later.

In many ways the Germanic sense of time is similar to that of Anglo-Americans. Generally, you should arrive on time for any event. Some Germans, however, follow a special rule for dinner invitations: guests should not arrive early or exactly at the appointed time so as not to appear too hungry. But otherwise, being fashionably late is not fashionable in the German-speaking countries.

In business situations, understanding the Germanic obsession with time is even more important. Not only should you be at the meeting on time, you'd better not try to change plans at the last minute. That violates the Germanic love of precise scheduling, and it throws everything out of kilter—not something that German-speakers appreciate.

Another important time-related cultural trait is the slower pace of things. This applies to getting an answer to a request, getting products delivered, and being served in a restaurant. For Americans the length of time required to get things done in the German culture can be frustrating. Americans have a "fast-food" sense of pace, while German speakers tend to have a more leisurely "four-course-dinner" concept of how long a given task should take. If the German store tells you the new dishwasher will be delivered in two weeks, it may take four (or longer). The decision you need from a business client may take longer than it would in the U.S. Although the Germans, Austrians, and Swiss may value punctuality (**Pünktlichkeit**), that does not always mean promptness (**Schnelligkeit**).

73. TRAINS

Traveling by train is the most common way of getting around in Europe (other than by car). **Deutsche Bahn AG**, the German Railway, Inc., known as German Rail in the English-speaking world, is one of Europe's most advanced rail systems. On a typical day, 350,000 passengers travel the long-distance routes of Deutsche Bahn, more than 64,000 of those in the popular new high-speed ICE trains.

Germany's very first train line, the Ludwigsbahn, was already running between Fürth and Nürnberg in 1835. However, Deutsche

Bahn has only been in existence since January 1994. Until that time, German trains had been run by two separate state-owned, deficit-ridden operations. The **Deutsche Bundesbahn** (DB) or German Federal Railway was the old West German railway that had been running things there since Germany's division in 1949. The **Deutsche Reichsbahn** (DR) or German Imperial Railway in former East Germany kept the pre-war name of the railroad that Hitler and those before him had known. The 1994 privatization was a merger of the two German state railroads that had tried to act as one since German reunification in 1990. However, the privatization was also an effort to get the government out from under billions of marks of mounting debt.

Since June 1991 the new ICE trains (InterCity Express) have been operating on several high-speed lines between major German cities like Berlin, Hamburg, Munich, Stuttgart, and Frankfurt. These sleek, white trains travel at 250-280 km/h (155-174 mph), whisking passengers along in quiet, comfortable cars equipped with video screens (in first class), stereo headsets, fax machines, and telephones. Like jet airplanes ICE cars are pressurized, sparing passengers any ear discomfort in the tunnels required to keep the roadbeds straight and level for high speed. The ICE has already knocked two hours off the old time to travel between Hamburg and Munich. The ICE now makes that trip in just five hours and 36 minutes, and as more of the high-speed roadbeds required by the ICE are built, that time will be cut even further. A third ICE line began service between Mannheim and Basel, Switzerland in the spring of 1993, although the final high-speed roadbed won't be ready until 2001 at the earliest. There are also new ICE links between Berlin and the western part of the country. Eventually, the German ICE will be part of a Europe-wide high-speed rail network.

Austria's state-owned **Österreichische Bundesbahnen** (**ÖBB**, Austrian Federal Railways) and Switzerland's **Schweizerische Bundesbahnen** (**SBB**, Swiss Federal Railways) have vast networks of rail lines in those countries. Switzerland also has several private railways, most of them in mountainous regions.

74. THE *Treuhand*

Before its dissolution in 1994, the **Treuhand** (TROY-hahnt) was responsible for the unpopular task of privatizing or liquidating the thousands of largely inefficient state concerns in former communist East Germany, a job that inevitably led to much criticism and controversy. Created on June 17, 1990 by joint action of the then two Germanys, the **Treuhand** was given a truly unique mission, one that no government agency had ever attempted to carry out before.

After the terrorist assassination of her predecessor in April 1991, Birgit Breuel took over as the new head of the **Treuhandanstalt** ("trustee agency"). Breuel, operating out of her Berlin headquarters, took on the daunting task of running the gigantic bureaucracy responsible for finding buyers for former East Germany's industrial and business concerns—14,000 of them, many of which were virtually bankrupt. About 20 percent of the concerns were sold to their employees or managers. The Treuhand also sold real estate and farmland, bringing the total of investment revenue and guarantees to more than DM 184 billion ($109 billion). About $13 billion of this money came from foreign investors, primarily from Austria, France, Switzerland, the United Kingdom, and the U.S. Some facilities were turned over to local governments.

The Treuhand faced criticism from all sides. Eastern Germans were unhappy about losing their jobs as their former concerns crumbled in the face of a true market economy. Western Germans complained about the DM 344 billion ($222 billion) of taxpayer money that the Treuhand expended during the four years of its existence. Balanced against a mere DM 74 billion ($48 billion) in sales revenue, the Treuhand ended up with a DM 270 billion deficit. Outside observers have expressed various opinions about the Treuhand's success or failure. Critics draw attention to bungling inefficiency, a lack of concern about keeping jobs, and overt corruption. Breuel admitted that there were problems, but defended her agency's efforts as the best that could be done under trying circumstances. Other Treuhand supporters pointed out that the real reason for some of the agency's problems was the failure to accurately assess the true state of the former East German economy. It was in far worse condition than anyone realized prior to 1990—the public sector was verging on bankruptcy, former eastern European markets were drying up, and the infrastructure was a total disaster. Added to all this, the Treuhand also had to deal with con artists and fraudulent offers.

The Treuhand may be history, but four successor agencies have taken on the task of resolving all the problems that have arisen in the world's largest reorganization. It will be many years before anyone can accurately assess the true state of the Treuhand's work.

75. THE WALL

By 1989 the Berlin Wall had become such an accepted and integral part of the Berlin environment that few Germans believed this ugly affront to humanity would ever come down, let alone in their lifetime. The true significance of this 98-mile-long structure of shame was almost lost amid the jubilation brought about by its demise on November 9, 1989. In the 28 years and almost three months since its construction on August 13, 1961, the Wall had become such a "part of the furniture" that many seemed to have forgotten what it had really done to the citizens of Berlin and Germany. On that infamous August night in 1961 families were suddenly divided, lovers separated, and friends cut off from each other—all because of an accident of geography and dependent on where in Berlin one happened to live.

In the sixties and early seventies, it still seemed possible that this insane assemblage of concrete block could disappear. One could see billboards and ads urging West Germans to keep their ties to the other side ("**Halte Verbindung nach drüben!**"). In the sixties, despite the Wall, there was still some hope that some day Germany would again be whole. But by the late seventies and eighties, despite the official West German plea of "**Mach das Tor auf!**" ("Open the gate!") and Allied insistence that the Wall had to come down—"Mr. Gorbachev, tear down this Wall!" (Reagan)—most Germans thought that reunification was very unlikely, if not impossible.

So the sudden collapse of the Wall in 1989 caught everyone off guard. Without seeming to realize the impact it would have, and in desperate reaction to increasing numbers of people fleeing to West Germany via Czechoslovakia, the GDR regime almost casually announced on the 5 p.m. evening news on November 9, 1989 that East Germans would be free to travel without restrictions. The announcement came so suddenly, it caught the border guards by surprise. As word spread that night, the border crossings were overwhelmed by a rising tide of East Germans rushing to visit West Berlin, most for the first time in their lives. Television showed the world images of Germans on both sides of the punctured Wall crying for joy. The exodus became so massive that East German border officials finally gave up any pretense of checking papers. In the next few days, additional openings were broken through a Wall that was fast disappearing. Americans could watch NBC's Tom Brokaw broadcasting from in front of the Wall at the Brandenburg Gate. By November 11, 1989, work began on opening the Wall at the famous **Potsdamer Platz**, which had been a desolate no-man's-land since 1961. The square was a bustling center of activity and heavy traffic before the war. On November 12th "opening" ceremonies were held with Willy Brandt, the former mayor of West Berlin, and other dignitaries. On November 13, 1989, the infamous **Schießbefehl**, the order to shoot people trying to escape across the East German "death strip," was finally rescinded. This empty gesture came only after 191 people had already been shot to death during escape attempts since 1961, several of them in the months just before the Berlin Wall and the 900-mile long fence along the inner-German border came down.

76. THE WC (*die Toilette*)

In German, a toilet is a **Toilette**. A **Badezimmer** is a bathroom. Never ask, "**Wo ist das Badezimmer?**" ("Where is the bathroom?") unless you intend to take a bath. If you want to use the facilities, just ask, "**Wo ist die Toilette, bitte?**" Euphemisms like "restroom" are not required. Public restrooms are labeled "**WC**" (water closet) or "**00.**" Ask for "**das WC**" (vay-say) or "**die Toilette**" (dee TOY-leta). "**Das Klo**" is another, less-refined, expression for the "john." Another term not used much any more, but still seen or heard once in a while is the "**Abort**"—roughly: the "away-place" (**ab/Ort**). Two of the first German words you should learn are **Damen** and **Herren** for "ladies" and "gentlemen"—sometimes indicated simply by a "D" or an "H."

Public restrooms all over the world are rarely models of good hygiene, and German ones tend to be as unpredictable as those in the States. One advantage not usually found in the U.S. is restroom attendants. Many public restrooms in Germany are maintained by male or female attendants. It can be a bit disconcerting for an American man standing at the urinal to have a German **Putzfrau** (cleaning lady) casually walk behind him, but it happens all the time and the restroom is usually nice and clean.

Attendants often have a dish sitting on a small table at the exit, suggesting that a small tip (**Trinkgeld**) would be appreciated. Leave a few 10-pfennig coins if you appreciate the cleanliness. (It's also a good way to get rid of the inevitable accumulation of coins.) The normal tip is about 50 pfennigs, and sometimes there is a sign in German listing the charges for the various "services"—using the urinal or the toilet, washing up with hot water, etc. There may be a mandatory charge to use some public restrooms in German-speaking countries. Often toilet stalls have a coin-operated lock that needs to be "fed" before you can gain access. Public restrooms in big-city train stations can be problem areas because of drug addicts and thieves.

77. WOMEN IN SOCIETY

Germany's 1949 constitution clearly states that women and men have equal rights. But in reality, as in many other parts of the world, women in Germany do not always enjoy those equal rights. Although the old-fashioned Germanic concept of **Kinder, Küche, Kirche** (children, kitchen, church) has not yet been entirely replaced by more enlightened thinking, women in Germany continue to make progress.

German women have been able to vote since 1918, but the intervening years added little to women's rights. Under the Third Reich in the 1930s and 1940s, women were seen more as producers and raisers of children, to the degree that abortion was punishable by death. Some women at the time, such as **Leni Riefenstahl** (1902-   ), a former actress, achieved success in certain areas, in her case as a famous pioneering film director for Hitler (*Olympia* and *Triumph of the Will*).

By 1957, legislation gave German women equal rights concerning joint property in a marriage. In 1977 German women and men could obtain a divorce without proving the guilt of the other party, and a divorcee was entitled to full pension benefits. Additional legislation in 1980 and 1994 added certain protection for women at work and prohibited gender-specific employment advertising. But laws and attitudes regarding women don't always agree. A recent survey revealed that sex discrimination was still present in 30 to 40 percent of help-wanted ads; only about half the ads for skilled workers and management positions were gender neutral. German women in general receive lower pay than their male counterparts, and find it more difficult to enter certain professions.

At the federal level, women hold only 6.7 percent of the executive positions in government agencies. Women head less than one in five of federal and state ministries combined, and those positions tend to be in the area of family, housing, and social welfare. The only **Land** with a female governor (**Ministerpräsidentin**) is Schleswig-Holstein. **Heide Simonis** (1943-   ) was elected to that position after the resignation of Björn Engholm in a political scandal. Simonis was also the German Secretary of the Treasury (**Finanz-Ministerin**) from 1988 to 1993. University professor **Rita Süßmuth** (1937-   ) has served as president of the German parliament (**Bundestag**) since 1988.

A recent survey indicated that women made up just 31.8 percent of the 1.45 million federal employees in German agencies, courts, the railroad, and the post office; the latter two departments have now been privatized. By comparison, women were more prevalent in federal jobs in eastern Germany. In the five new **Länder** women made up 41.7 percent of the federal workforce, while in western Germany a mere 28.6 percent was female. The post office (**Deutsche Post AG**) led the way in hiring women with 41.4 percent, but in eastern Germany females were a dominant 61.2 percent of postal employees. In 1992, women held only one out of eight leadership positions overall in the federal government; this was a slight improvement over 1989 when women held only one in ten of leadership positions. The German Ministry for Women and Youth was created in 1991.

Although Austrian women have had the right to vote since 1918, they have had to wait until recent years to achieve any degree of true equality. Abortion was illegal until 1974. Since the 1970s Austrian women have made rapid progress towards more equality. An "Equal Rights Act" and an "Equal Rights Commission" came into effect in 1979, and a 1985 amendment outlawed sex bias in job advertising. In 1990 a female "Attorney for Equal Rights" was appointed to help women who file discrimination charges.

Swiss women have only had the right to vote in federal elections since 1971. Before 1971, women in some Swiss cantons could vote in local and cantonal elections. It was 1984 before the first woman was elected to Switzerland's executive body, the seven-member **Bundesrat** (Federal Council). Because of ethics charges (later dropped), Elisabeth Kopp was forced to resign in 1989. In 1993, another woman, Ruth Dreifuss (1940-   ), was elected to a four-year term. She holds the position of Minister of the Interior.

The tiny Principality of Liechtenstein (**Fürstentum Liechtenstein**), tucked in between Austria and Switzerland, was the last holdout on women's suffrage in the German-speaking world. The women of Liechtenstein finally gained the right to vote in 1984.

For updates, expanded information, photos, and Web links related to the 77 points in this book, visit *The German Way* Web site at **www.german-way.com/german/**.

BIBLIOGRAPHY

Ardagh, John. *Germany and the Germans: An Anatomy of Society Today* (New York: Harper & Row, 1987)

Barzini, Luigi. *The Europeans* (New York: Penguin, 1983)

Borneman, John. *After the Wall* (New York: Basic, 1991)

Craig, Gordon A. *The Germans* (New York: G.P. Putnam's Sons, 1982)

Darnton, Robert. *Berlin Journal: 1989-1990* (New York: W.W. Norton, 1991)

Fisher, Marc. *After the Wall: Germany, the Germans and the Burdens of History* (New York: Simon & Schuster, 1995).

Hall, Edward T. and Mildred Reed Hall. *Understanding Cultural Differences: Germans, French and Americans* (Yarmouth, Maine: Intercultural Press, 1990)

Marsh, David. *The Germans: A People at the Crossroads* (New York: St. Martin's Press, 1990)

Miller, Stuart. *Understanding Europeans* (Santa Fe: John Muir, 1990)

Mog, Paul and Hans-Joachim Althaus. *Die Deutschen in ihrer Welt: Tübinger Modell einer integrativen Landeskunde* (Berlin: Langenscheidt, 1992)

Pattee, Dee. *Munich in Your Pocket: How to Become a Münchner* (Munich: D.C. Pattee, 1994)

Schneider, Peter. *The German Comedy: Scenes of Life After the Wall* (New York: Farrar, Straus, and Giroux, 1991) [translation of the original German: *Extreme Mittellage: Eine Reise durch das deutsche Nationalgefühl*, Rowohlt, 1990.]

Stern, Susan, Ed. *Meet United Germany* (Frankfurt: Atlantik-Brücke, 1992)

Stern, Susan. *These Strange German Ways* (Bonn: Atlantik-Brücke, 1995)

Wiedemann, Erich. *Die deutschen Ängste: Ein Volk in Moll* (Frankfurt: Ullstein, 1990)

Wolfe, Tom. *From Bauhaus to Our House* (New York: Farrar Straus Giroux, 1981)

INDEX

INDEX

INDEX